A MAP OF THE UNIVERSE

A MAP OF THE UNIVERSE

An Introduction to the Study of Kabbalah

Rabbi Max Weiman

Copyright © 2003 by Rabbi Max Weiman.

Library of Congress Number: 2003090935
ISBN :   Hardcover   1-4010-9656-5
            Softcover   1-4010-9655-7

All rights reserved. No part of this book may be reproduced or transmitted in any form or by any means, electronic or mechanical, including photocopying, recording, or by any information storage and retrieval system, without permission in writing from the copyright owner.

This book was printed in the United States of America.

To order additional copies of this book, contact:
Xlibris Corporation
1-888-795-4274
www.Xlibris.com
Orders@Xlibris.com

18065

CONTENTS

Acknowledgements 9
Preface 11

Chapter One	What is Kabbalah, and Why is it a Secret?	15
Chapter Two	Man is a Microcosm of the Universe	23
Chapter Three	Israel, the Torah, and God Are All One	29
Chapter Four	The Purpose of Creation is to Be One with God	35
Chapter Five	Our World is Traveling Towards Its Destiny	41
Chapter Six	The Spiritual World Responds to the Physical World	47
Chapter Seven	All of Mankind is Interwoven and Interdependent	55
Chapter Eight	Good and Bad Things Happen to All People	61
Chapter Nine	Life is Filled with Challenges, Lessons, and "Tikkunim"	67
Chapter Ten	The Letters of the Hebrew Alphabet are the Building Blocks of Creation	73

In Conclusion 79
Notes 81
Index 87
About the author 105
Biblical Sources Quoted 89
Classical Sources of the Oral Tradition Quoted in
  "Map of the Universe" 91
Biographical Notes on Well Known Kabbalists 95
Glossary of Hebrew Terms 99

This book is dedicated to Jess, Dude, Betz, Koob, Daniel, Burt, and Arthur . . . wherever the heck they may be.

ACKNOWLEDGEMENTS

The Almighty has been exceedingly kind with me by allowing me to be involved with Torah, and giving me so many blessings.

Thanks to my wife, Chava, for her support and inspiration.

All of my students help me clarify what I study by asking questions, and by forcing me to articulate the ideas I teach.

My colleagues help me by challenging my assumptions, and being a sounding board for ideas. In particular, I have been helped in this way by Rabbi Elazar Grunberger, Rabbi Shmuel Greenwald, Rabbi Gidon Nitsun, and Rabbi Ari Kahn.

My teachers gave me a methodology and an approach to Torah study that is beyond value. In particular, I would like to thank Rabbi Noah Weinberg, Rabbi Shlomo Rothenberg, and Rabbi Yitzchak Berkovitz. As well, I have been inspired by Rabbi Noah Orlowek and Rabbi Zelig Pliskin.

Thanks also to the fabulous support staff and volunteers of Aish St. Loius: Albert Glassman, editors Vickie Lecy, JoAnn Turner, and Tracy Bernstein, not to mention the computer and web work of Dovid Lecy and Lon Bliss.

Thanks to the staff at Xlibris.

PREFACE

Often people look for something unusual to teach them about that which is usual. This is what brought me into Harry's Occult Shop in Philadelphia, PA one sunny day in 1982. I didn't realize it at the time, but I was looking for some truth about the world amidst the shrunken heads, incense, candles, and love potions in this dark musky store. Harry, a large muscular man with tattoos and a menacing look, was incongruously as nice and helpful as my neighborhood fish salesman in the nearby Italian market south of South Street. My only purchase from Harry was a book that fascinated me on Hebrew numerology. This was my introduction to Kabbalah. It wasn't until years later after much study that I realized that the author of that book really didn't have much knowledge of Kabbalah.

    A year ago I began writing a series of essays as an introduction to the study of Kabbalah. It became apparent that they could be put together to form a book, and numerous people had asked for such a book. Anyone searching for truths in the world of Jewish mysticism will now have an introduction to that study to make their time better spent. The ideas presented in this book lay the groundwork for all advanced concepts in Kabbalah. They are the fundamentals. Before someone can truly understand things like angels, magic, and spiritual forces, he/she needs some background. This is it.

Certainly the kabbalists who are considered masters of this information know and understand clearly the five books of Moses, the eight major and twelve minor books of the prophets, the eleven books called Writings, as well as the sixty tractates of the Talmud, (the compendium of Jewish Law that was originally an oral tradition, written down about 500 C.E.)[1] There is much more to know than what is in this small book. To become a master kabbalist takes many years of study with proper teachers. This book is a jump-start to grasp essential ideas and perhaps some sophisticated concepts.

At this time there is an unprecedented desire for spirituality spreading throughout the world. For many, Kabbalah is filling that desire. Human beings need meaning. We know there's more to the world than meets the eye. Our generation in particular is groping for the spiritual realm. There are those that suggest this is a fulfillment of the prophecy in Amos 8:11 that refers to a "hunger not for bread" that will come to the world.[2] And there are those that say it's merely a reaction people have nowadays to feeling overwhelmed by technology.

Books written by people who know little actual Kabbalah, and understand even less, are filling the market. They are not the answer. On the other hand, for the neophyte to turn to the older works is nearly impossible, since the traditional works are difficult to understand and rarely translated. Therefore the hope is that this book will fill in part of the gap of knowledge for many. What is presented here is footnoted and based on traditional classical works of Kabbalah. Biographical notes and explanations of Hebrew terms are added at the end of the book.

There are so many people that are thirsting for this knowledge that have been unable to attain it. May it be God's will that this book serves as a way for them to taste the essence of their traditions, and makes them thirsty for more.

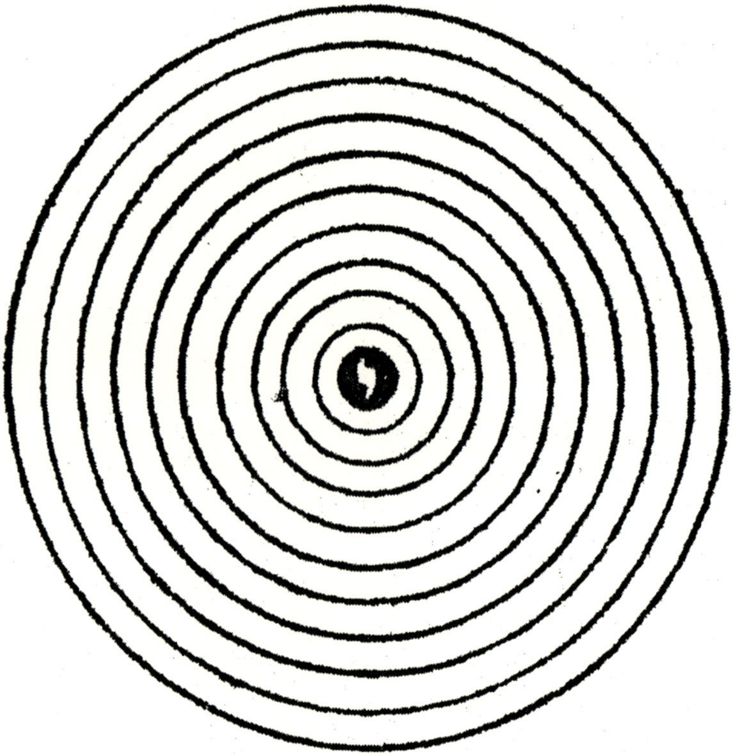

CHAPTER ONE

What is Kabbalah, and Why is it a Secret?

> *"The crooked one is abhorred by God, but to the righteous He reveals His secrets."*
> Proverbs 3:32

Kabbalah is most easily defined as Jewish mysticism; it has information about the spiritual realm, reincarnation, white magic, and meditation. But this definition is somewhat deceiving, as it doesn't put this ancient study in its proper context. Judaism, the religion of the Jews, is divided into two parts: the Written Law and the Oral Law. God gave both to Moses on Mount Sinai. The Written Law includes the five books of Moses, the books of the Prophets, and the Writings, (Psalms, Proverbs, etc.). The Oral Law includes the Talmud, the Medrash, and Kabbalah. In other words, Kabbalah is one section of the oral tradition of the Jews. Yet it is also used to elucidate and give deeper meaning to all the other parts of Judaism.[3]

Although the majority of the oral law has been written down, it was meant to be transmitted only orally, and many ideas are still kept alive only from teacher to student. It is said that, in general, *Jewish law[4] describes how man relates to God, and Kabbalah describes how God relates to man.* Kabbalah gives us a deeper look at everything in existence and gives us a "why" behind many of the rituals in Judaism that do not have a rational ethic behind them. There are many customs and "superstitions" that are based on Kabbalah. It has always been around, and has had both positive and negative effects on the Jews as a nation throughout history.

Kabbalah in Hebrew means "to receive". Why is Jewish mysticism called Kabbalah? One reason may be that which Rabbi Moshe Chaim Luzzatto[5] writes in *The Way of God* 1:5:2, "The properties of the physical world are known to us, the physical laws in general are well known. The spiritual realm, however, is impossible to picture and its properties are beyond our intellect. We can only speak about them from tradition." Since knowledge of the spiritual realm is not derived purely from scripture, nor deduced from logic, we are forced to rely solely on tradition to teach us about it. That tradition can be traced from God to Moses, Moses to Joshua, to the Elders, Prophets, Men of the Great Assembly, etc.[6] teacher to student throughout the ages.[7] Therefore Kabbalah is not something you discern, its something you receive.

A teaching from the Mishna[8] shows us two categories of mystical teachings. "We don't expound upon the Act of Creation to more than one person. We don't expound upon the Chariot to even one person, unless it is a wise man who understands on his own."[9] The first category, called the Act of Creation, or "Maaseh Beraishis" in Hebrew, is what comprises most of the kabbalistic writings. It is a description of the structure of the spiritual world and how it interfaces with the physical universe as was designed in God's act of creation. The second category, called the Act of the Chariot, or "Maaseh Merkavah" in Hebrew, is the way to meditate on the spiritual forces through permutations of God's names.[10] The word "merkavah" also means permutation. The first category is also referred to as Theoretical Kabbalah. The second category is often broken into two: Meditative Kabbalah, and Practical Kabbalah.

In general, Kabbalah is traditionally a secret or hidden doctrine. Why? Powerful ideas are not always understood correctly by the masses. A misunderstanding about the nature of the universe is more dangerous than a misunderstanding about the laws of theft or property damage. Basic law can be taught publicly, but not mysticism. Also the ability to do spiritual damage is great when equipped with the knowledge of the fabric of the spiritual realm. For these reasons and others, Kabbalah has been kept largely with only the most accomplished sages. Furthermore, there are kabbalistic meditations that are very dangerous to the practitioner, even for advanced scholars. An incident related in the Talmud expresses this point:

> *Four sages entered the "orchard." They are Ben Azai, Ben Zoma, The Other, and Rabbi Akiva. Rabbi Akiva told them, "When you come near the pure marble stone don't say 'water, water' because it says in Psalms 101:7 'The one who speaks falsely cannot remain in front of my eyes.'" Ben Azai stared and died. Of him it is applicable the verse, "Dear in the eyes of God is the*

death of His righteous ones." Psalms 116:15. *Ben Zoma stared and became stricken. And of him the verse is applicable, "Have you found honey? Eat only what you need, lest you be satiated and vomit."* Proverbs 25:16 *The Other 'cut the plantings*[11]*." Rabbi Akiva left unhurt.*[12]

The "orchard"[13] is a code word for kabbalistic meditation. All four were sages. Ben Azzai died because the spiritual experience forced his soul to leave his body. Ben Zoma became deranged because his mind was not strong enough to handle the change in reality. The unnamed scholar, known as Other, became a heretic because his vision of the spiritual realm was not in consonance with his understanding of God. Only one sage, Rabbi Akiva, went into the meditation and came out of the meditation unscathed. So we see its safer not to enlighten the masses. The information will find its way to the ones who are equipped to receive it. God runs the world, and He has His ways of getting the right people the knowledge they deserve.

On the other hand, there is a world of mystical and spiritual ideas that are part of the average person's knowledge and understanding. These ideas are not kept hidden; they were part of the sages' daily discourses and often make up a major part of someone's basic religious knowledge. The Kabbalah, being part of the Oral Tradition, is one of the ways the Written Tradition is explained. In general, this is the function of the Oral Tradition, namely, to explain what is written. Without an oral explanation much of the Bible and Prophetic writings are easily misunderstood, or not understood at all. How would you know what an angel or a soul is?

How would you know what the next world is all about? It's also not always possible to draw a line between a practical, philosophical, ethical and mystical interpretation of a verse. These areas often overlap. Therefore the world of Kabbalah is not completely closed off from us.

Surprisingly, in recent generations, the "forbidden" parts of Kabbalah have been opened up to those that want to know. Rabbi Shneur Zalman of Liadi explains, "The Zohar[14] was hidden in the Talmudic times, and also all the wisdom of Kabbalah was concealed, and removed from all sages except a select few. And even then it wasn't taught publicly, as the Talmud says. Therefore it was stated by Rabbi Isaac Luria that only in recent generations is it permissible and even a mitzvah to reveal this wisdom, not as in earlier generations."[15] It also says in the book *Leshem Shebo Veachlama*, "Rabbi Luria revealed the secrets of Maaseh Berashis and Maaseh Merkavah; they were known to him like all the simple matters of the Torah. He opened up these secrets, and permission was given to anyone engaged in this study to understand, each according to his ability. Especially from the year 5600(1840 c.e.) and onward, as it says in the Zohar . . ."[16] Even so, mysticism is still referred to as the "wine" in the banquet of Jewish learning. As my teacher put it, "Too much wine on an empty stomach and *zinnnng!*"[17]

Even the hidden ideas, though, have many aspects that are taught in parables or analogies that can be understood both simply and deeply. For example the study of Kabbalah itself is explained in the beginning of the Zohar, which is the most famous compendium of Kabbalah. In the introduction of the Zohar, Rabbi Shimon explains that the five books of Moses contain three basic elements: the stories, the commandments, and the meaning behind it all. The stories are like the clothing of a man, they tell you about the man but they are not the man at all. The commandments are like the body of a man; they are the real man, yet they are still not his essence. The meaning behind it all, i.e. Kabbalah, is like the soul of a man. That is the true man, the essence and most important part of him. If someone only reads the stories and defines the commandments, they have missed the essence of the five books of Moses.

The Hebrew word for Bible is Torah, which means "teaching" or "instruction." The Torah is God's teaching to humanity. The reason why scholars have studied the Kabbalah for so long is because they are convinced that God taught these ideas to man. Without a conviction in God, there is little reason anymore to study Kabbalah. Hence piety and advanced study of Kabbalah has historically gone hand in hand. Although no human being is perfect or infallible, the earlier great kabbalists were known as pious and scholarly individuals. If one of the individuals left the path of observance, he would lose his following. Belief in one, all-powerful, infinite Being is not merely a prerequisite to a true understanding of Judaism; it is also the basis of all Kabbalistic ideas. In fact, the study of Kabbalah is often called "chochmas Elokus," which means the wisdom of Godliness.

Given the understanding above that Kabbalah is part of the Oral Tradition, you might assume that the Written Tradition does not have mystical ideas in it. However, many mystical ideas are hinted to throughout the written law. There are passages in the Bible that beg for explanation, including the section where Moses asks to see more of God.[18] A more obviously mystical passage is the beginning of the book of the prophet Ezekiel, the prophet, which contains fantastic mystical allusions.[19] In addition, more basic mystical ideas like the messiah, the resurrection of the dead, the soul and the afterlife are popular topics in the Prophets, Psalms, and other writings.

In summary, Kabbalah is the Hebrew word which means to receive. There is wisdom that is learned through hard study. There is wisdom that is understood through experience. But most mystical or spiritual understandings of our reality can only be "received'. This implies that the recipient must be ready for, and be a fitting vessel for receiving such special and holy ideas. No matter what a book has to offer, the ability to absorb, grasp, understand, and retain depends on the work the student or reader does to become a fitting vessel. This is emphasized in the verse, "The secrets of God (are given) to those who are in awe of Him."[20]

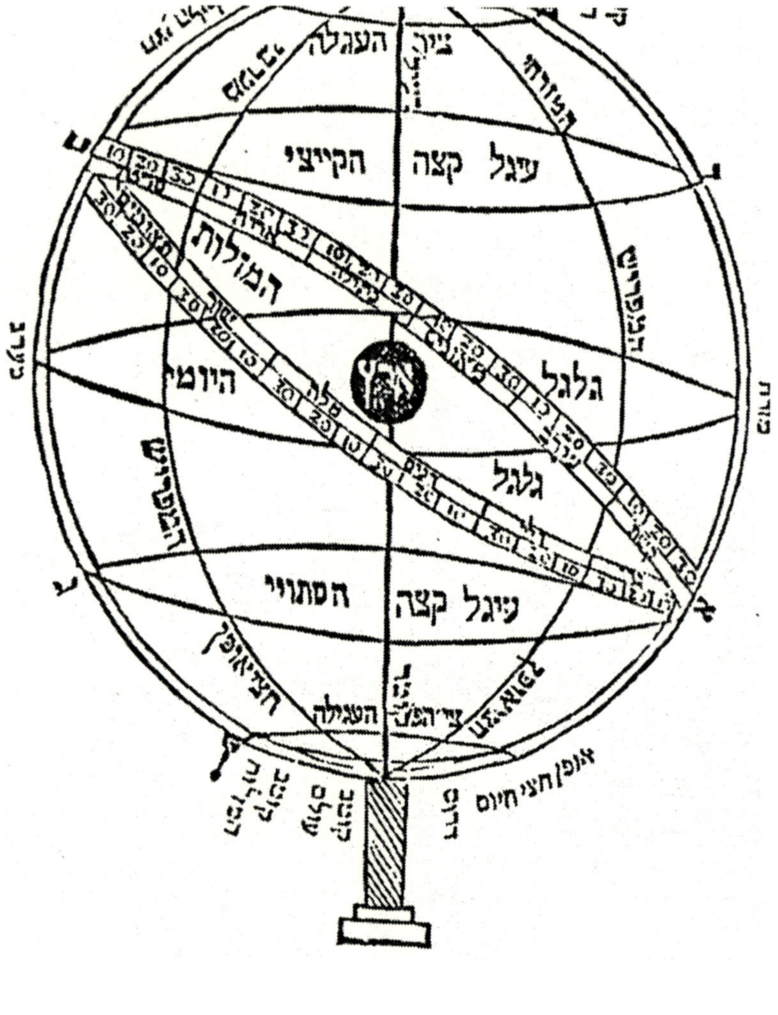

עיגל קצה הקייצי
עיגל קצה הסתווי
גלגל
גלגל
המזלות
היומי
העגלה
העגלה
אופן חצי חיום

CHAPTER TWO

Man is a Microcosm of the Universe

> *"When I look at your heavens, your handiwork, the moon and the stars that you affixed; what is man that you notice us, and the son of man that you command us, yet you made us a little less than God, and crowned us with honor and glory."*
>
> Psalms 8:4-6

In the previous chapter we focused on the concept of God as the essence of Kabbalistic study. Any reference to God in Kabbalah is a deeper concept than most of us are used to when discussing God in a biblical context. Many people have the same notion of God they did when they were a child. It's easy to misunderstand the anthropomorphism in the Bible. They live with a confused idea of a "vengeful" God; a God who waits to punish for wrongdoing. While walking through a hotel lobby in the Catskills I overheard a woman telling a friend, "When I was young, the first time I broke Shabbos I thought a lightening bolt would come out of the sky to strike me dead!" This is a childish version of the Infinite Being. God is beyond our comprehension yet acts as a loving father who only wants what's best for His children. His chastisement is to teach us what is in our own best interest. He is infinite and needs nothing. He doesn't benefit from our good deeds, nor suffer from our transgressions. It's all for our benefit. An intelligent person realizes that God has no gender, is non-corporeal, and all the references to God "seeing" or "getting angry" in the Bible is allegorical. In Kabbalah the references get even more sophisticated. He is infinite and the physical references are symbolic of mystical concepts. Every name of God means something different.

In order to fully grasp how this is the whole point of kabbalistic study, there are other foundational concepts that must be understood first. They will be the subjects of these nine chapters. They are the basic concepts that are part and parcel of so many advanced ideas. The idea of this chapter is a deeper look at man. Just as God is looked at on a deeper level, so is man.

Without the idea of man as a microcosm much further knowledge will be hard to put into context. The reader is asked not only to grasp this concept, but also to expand it and connect it wherever he/she is able. Then the other pieces of the puzzle will be put together. This must be done with every concept mentioned. How do they put pieces of the puzzle together? Imagine someone understanding electricity for the first time. Suddenly, all the electrical appliances in the house start to make sense, how they work, why their plugs are dangerous, what outlets are etc. Similarly, the more advanced mystical wisdom will be better understood better after knowing the concepts presented in these chapters. Because you are a microcosm of the universe, you really have all of this knowledge deeply embedded in your subconscious. All you are doing now is allowing it to come forward. There is a related story mentioned in the Talmud[21] describing how a fetus in the womb is taught all the wisdom of the Torah. Upon birth, an angel touches the child on the upper lip and all is forgotten. It remains in our subconscious. That way when we come across truth, it's like being reminded of something you once knew.

In the Talmud, man is referred to as an "olam", a small universe. "Man was created alone to teach you that one who kills a single Jewish soul is as if he destroyed an entire universe, and one who saves a single Jewish soul is as if he saves an entire universe."[22] This is one reference to the idea we are touching on. Man embodies vastly different elements brought together to form a unit. As you read this, the physical world and the spiritual realm are tied together by you, a finite being, reaching out to the infinite. You do this because God fused those two realms together when He formed man. We are both a symbol and also an expression of the very fabric of all creation. We are at once both physical and spiritual.

On the physical side, the human body contains the four basic elements of creation, which are water, air, fire, and earth. The body is mostly water yet it doesn't leak; it knows how and when to release liquid from itself. It is also surprisingly waterproof, rain rolls right off. We can produce a kind of wind from our lungs. There is a natural heat within us. Lastly, God in Genesis 2:7 said that He created man from the dust of the ground. We see water, air, fire, and earth, all four primordial elements of creation in man.

The combination of the soul and the body is also a

symbol. Man's soul in the body parallels God's presence in the universe. The soul fills the body just as God's presence fills the universe.[23] The soul is the life-giver to the body, just as God is the life-giver to the universe. Judaism teaches that God didn't just make the universe and leave it; He constantly wills it to exist. The soul is the only reason for the body's existence, the body exists to serve the soul, and similarly the universe exists to serve its creator. The soul cannot be seen, yet you know it is there, just as God can't be seen yet we know He is there. This is one way of understanding the verse in the Torah when God said, "Let us make man in our image."[24] This means that there are a number of similarities in the way God manifests Himself in our world and how the soul manifests itself in the body. This is elaborated upon in the kabbalistic work Nefesh HaChaim, quoting the Zohar "When God made man, He arranged in him all of the aspects of the secrets of the upper realms, and all the aspects of the secrets of the lower realms. All is carved into the spiritual blueprint of man who stands in the 'image of God.'"[25]

Another basic understanding of the kabbalists is that man is interwoven with the universe in a way that causes the entire universe to be spiritually elevated when man elevates himself, and lowered when man lowers himself. For example, if you give a poor person some money, or a job, you have changed yourself, molded yourself to be a little bit more like the Almighty. You have increased the positive energy in the world, and removed some of its negativity. Beyond this, because you are interwoven with the fabric of the universe, you have elevated not only yourself, but also the entire creation. There is now more mercy and kindness in all of creation. We see this stated in the classic ethical treatise by the kabbalist

Luzzatto, "If man is drawn after the physical world and distances himself from his Creator, he is ruined and the world is ruined with him. If he controls his nature and clings to his Creator, and uses the world only as a means to serve his Creator, then he elevates himself and the world itself is elevated with him."[26]

To conclude, in advanced Kabbalah there are many references to spiritual limbs, analogies to the human form, and conceptual links to personality traits, gender, and the body. These can be grasped more clearly when viewed through the perspective of man as a microcosm. All the spiritual realms are contained in man. All wisdom is contained in man. This "microcosm" concept will come up explicitly and implicitly in the rest of the book.

קמיע לחן

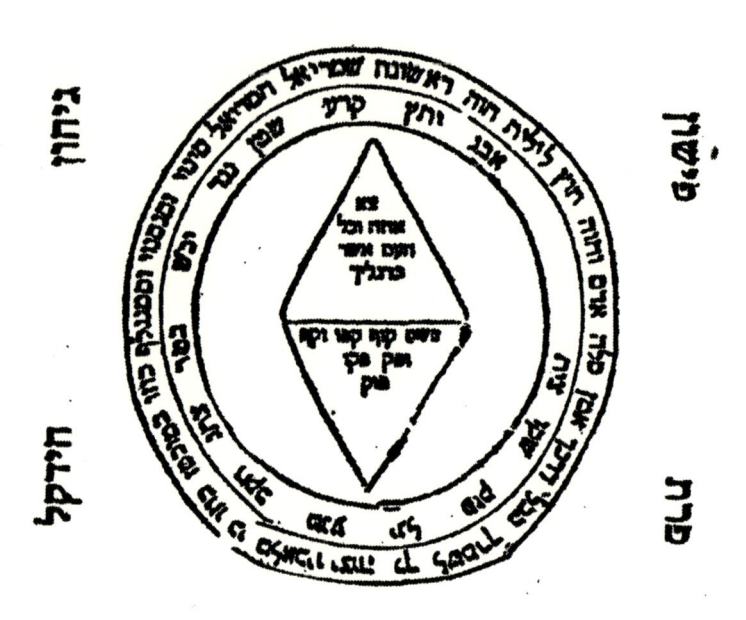

קמיע לשלום

קמיע לחכמה

קמיע לרוח

CHAPTER THREE

Israel, the Torah, and God Are All One

"And God will be king over all the world; on that day God will be one and His name will be one."
Zechariah 14:9

It is written in the book Nefesh HaChaim, "The main life force, light and continuity of all the universes depends on our acting properly, since God, the Torah, and Israel are as one, as the root of every Jewish soul is tied to a letter of the Torah, and they become one."[27]

Israel is not a race. The status of being an Israelite, after the revelation at Mt. Sinai, only passes through the mother, not the father. Therefore it's not a race. Israel is not a religion. If you do not believe in Judaism, you don't lose the status of being an Israelite. If you are not born Jewish and adopt a belief in Judaism, you still do not have the status of an Israelite. As a side point, one can believe every major idea in Judaism and still chose to remain a righteous gentile within the Jewish religion. That gentile will receive a reward in the world to come. No one has a *guarantee* of a portion in the next world, of course, even an Israelite. It all depends on one's deeds.

Israel is a spiritual definition of a soul that has a specific obligation to all the commandments in the Torah. All who stood on Mt.Sinai at the Revelation achieved this status. They all were considered converts. Since then, a gentile can become a convert through a formal conversion that includes acceptance of all the commandments, immersion in a ritual bath in the presence of three designated Rabbis, and circumcision (if male). A child born to an Israelite woman attains this status automatically.

In the previous chapter, we discussed the idea of man being a microcosm of the universe. In one sense everything in creation mirrors man and vice versa. The point of creation, however, was just for man, and therefore he has more importance than the animals, plants, rocks, or cosmos.[28] More importance than the angels, and spiritual realms or forces. The universe is the arena in which man fulfills his divine task. The vehicle to communicate that task to man is the Torah. Although the word Torah can refer to the actual scroll of the Bible, it also refers to the entirety of God's instructions to man. As we said before, there are the written instructions, which include the five books of Moses, the Prophets, and the Writings; as well as the oral instructions, which include the Mishna, Medrash, Talmud, and Kabbalah. Therefore the word "Torah" in the chapter title can refer to the entirety of *knowledge* that is imbedded in the five books of Moses.

As instructions to man, the Torah represents the very will of the Creator. Knowing His will is the closest we can come to knowing Him. It's the next best thing to

God's actual presence. We can't come face to face with God, as it says in Exodus 33:20 " . . . for no man can see me and live." In this way we say that God and the Torah are one, as it is the greatest manifestation or revelation of God we have here on earth. In the Zohar, the Torah is even referred to as one long name of God.[29] In a matter of speaking it is His very words, thoughts, and desires.

During the short time I was engaged to my wife I went to Israel to study. I only had a few photographs of her that she gave me before I left. Those pictures became so precious to me because they were the closest I could feel to being with her. Similarly, the Torah is precious as it is the closest thing to being with God.

If you think about it, you realize that the creation itself is also an expression of God as well. He created it. It is His handiwork, and it has His wisdom all the way through it. He made the apple pretty to look at, a pleasure to smell, delicious and healthy to eat. If one examines the universe properly one will come to the unmistakable conclusion that there is a Creator and designer; it could not have been an accident. The earth is just the right distance from the sun for viable life. Trees grow leaves in the spring when we begin to need the shade, and drop them in the fall when we start to need the warmth of the sunlight. The list goes on and on. Psychologists sometimes examine great works of art or literature, and draw conclusions about the artist or writer. With the creation, though, God purposely designed His universe to hide Himself just a bit beneath the surface. If you look hard, you will notice Him in every breath you take. Since God's oneness fills the universe and constantly wills it into existence, the universe is more like a living self-portrait, albeit with just a thin veil to gaze past.

We are part of His creation. Man is the most important and special thing God created, and thereby the greatest expression of His will. Man also, as a microcosm of all creation, is a representation of the whole of God's will as manifested in the world. So just as the universe and the Torah are fused and connected with God, so is man. Yet it is man in his fulfillment of the purpose of creation that best expresses the presence of God. Therefore the formation of this nation called Israel is the embodiment of God's will and as a people they continue this role throughout history. They are the people charged with the task to follow His instructions. Israel is the name given to Jacob, the third of the Jewish patriarchs, when he wrestled with an angel in Genesis 32:29 (see also 35:10). The name Israel also refers to the Jewish people as a whole. They were formed as a people from Abraham's time until Moses, and were established with God's mandate on Mount Sinai. Historians have noticed that this nation implies a divine connection.

"The author has deliberately attempted to write this work in a secular spirit; he does not think that his readers can fail to see in it, on every page, a higher immanence." Cecil Roth, *A History of the Jews*, Oxford University

"Its survival is a mysterious and wonderful phenomenon demonstrating that the life of this people is governed by a special predetermination, transcending the processes of adaptation expounded by the materialistic interpretation of history." Professor Nicholai Berdysev, Moscow Academy of Spiritual Culture.

Israel, as it lives the principles of the Torah, becomes a living expression of God's will in man. They are the people that were given the instructions, and they are the ones who are living those instructions. Israel, the Torah and God are all one.

The normal and natural way of viewing an object that exists outside of oneself is to consider it an independent and separate item. This is why growing up your natural inclination is to view God, the Torah, and yourself as three distinct and separate items. It is a slightly mind-bending experience when you recognize that what you thought were two separate things become one, or vice versa. This was part of the beauty of the Performance Art of the seventies and eighties when the artist became the art piece. A similar feeling erupts when you see an actor in a movie wink at the camera, and break the illusion of the audience's non-existence, like in Harold and Maude, and some Woody Allen movies. Throughout the Kabbalah it happens that one realm of thought bleeds into another. One realm of existence blends into another. This is what happens with God and the creation. The Artist, His paints, and the painting share enough elements to become one, as Maimonides says, "He is the knower, He is the knowledge, He is the power to know."[30]

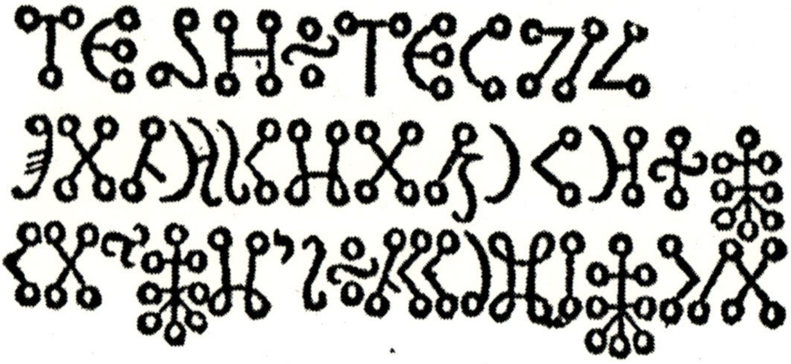

CHAPTER FOUR

The Purpose of Creation is to Be One with God

"And God said to Moses, 'Tell the entire congregation of Israel the following, "You shall be holy, for I am holy, your God."'"
Leviticus 19:1,2

We are born a lump of clay. Our mission is to mold that clay into the shape of holiness. Practical and mystical Judaism converge on this point. Man's most essential question as a living human being is "Why are we here?" Every thinking person must ask this question sooner or later. The cartoons frequently depict a stereotype of a person climbing a mountain to reach a thin, bearded man who the climber asks, "Oh wise one, what is the meaning of life?" To which he answers something enigmatic like "Life is like the hole inside a doughnut." If you believe in God, the answer is right in front of you. You don't need to travel or climb a mountain. As it says, "For this commandment that I command you today, it is not hidden from you, and it is not distant from you."[31] The Torah's answer to this question is the very heart and soul of everything in the Torah. What could possibly be the point of all the Biblical commandments if they don't fulfill this purpose? We often view the commandments as being a set of rules for a healthy society, and they certainly are. Society is more civilized when no one steals, kills, rapes, etc. They are good for society, but that is the most superficial level of the Torah. They do so much more.

There are 613 commandments in the Torah.[32] Each one is a conduit or method of becoming one with God. We see that cleaving to God or imitating God is a general theme in the Torah, as it says in Deuteronomy 10:12, " . . . what does God, your Lord, ask of you? To be in awe of God, your Lord, to walk in His ways . . ." It also says in Deut. 11:22, " . . . love God, your Lord, to walk in His ways and to cling to Him."[33] Philosophically speaking, the intention of the Creator in His creation was to give another being the greatest possible good and ultimate pleasure.[34] As God is the source of infinite good and bliss, the greatest possible good and pleasure is to be a part of Him. To be given this good without any effort would be lacking in the essential quality of God that He Himself was not given goodness. The closest we can come to being like God, then, is to earn our closeness to Him.

That defines the purpose of our creation, but not the method. The method of us earning this greatest good is the struggle in a realm seemingly devoid of God, and striving to be one with Him. By fulfilling the commandments we are perfecting ourselves, emulating God, and becoming one with God all at the same time. The period of struggle is a finite one; that's what we call "this world." The period of experiencing what we have accomplished is infinite; that's what we call "the World to Come."[35] In the end we must come out of the realm of illusion where God is not apparent, and go into the realm of reality. This world is illusory; the world to come is real. This destroys the Hollywood stereotype of heaven. Heaven is not a place to get paid for doing good things. It is a place to come to a realization of the Godliness that a person developed in this realm.

One act of goodness done by us, a simple "Have a nice day" when said with sincerity, makes us more Godly, and brings more Godliness into the world. From a spiritual perspective, each commandment is a way of making God's oneness more evident in the world. The kabbalists even have a short phrase to say before the performance of a mitzvah to remind them of this, which translates as "For the sake of unifying the Holy One, Blessed is He with His Divine Presence, through He who is hidden and unseen."[36] Many of the commandments are easily mistaken as mere ritual. However, every so-called ritual act that God requests from us is actually a mystical connection that binds the soul to its source, the Infinite One. That's why it's possible for the commentaries to say that the forefathers kept the commandments before the revelation on Mt. Sinai.[37] For example, on Passover we eat matzah ostensibly as a symbol of the exodus from Egypt. The mystical sources say that Abraham, who lived many years before the exodus, also ate matzah on the night that would one day be called Passover. He saw past the surface to the spiritual benefit that lies beneath. The matzah is an expression of humility. The power of the holiday is the ability to nullify ourselves to God's will. This power is enhanced and activated through the mitzvah of the matzah, which is like a spiritual injection meant to last until the next year. The forefathers' level of spirituality was so strong they didn't need to be told to eat matzah on that night in the month of Nissan. Through reason, prayer, and intuition they recognized the mystical significance of all the commandments, and fulfilled them without being told to do so.

Why did God create the universe? If He is infinite, then He needs nothing. It could not have been to fill any need or lack in Him. It must be that creation was done for the sake of the created. In order for the created to experience the ultimate gift it must face moral challenges, and struggle to cling to spirituality. This is the way to become Godlike. We need a universe in which to experience these challenges. We need to have the potential for good and evil both inside and out. Why are there people starving in the world? So we will feed them. Why is there evil in the world? So we will fight it. God's presence also must be somewhat hidden in the world lest we be forced by the awe of being in front of Him. The word in Hebrew for universe is "haolam". This word also means "that which is hidden". God doesn't need robots. The essence of our existence is in using our free will to come closer to God. When it says in the Torah, "Let us make man in our image,"[38] that image is the free will to choose right or wrong.

There is nothing superfluous in the Torah. There is nothing extra in the world. For every human endeavor whether its work, sleep, sex, eating, or anything else, there is a principle of spirituality that the Torah teaches regarding that endeavor. There is a way to elevate the act. All physicality can be used for spirituality. With this in mind the Torah can be used as a spiritual encyclopedia. Whatever human activity you want to do, you can look up a principle that elevates the act to a spiritual experience. Man's life experiences and personality are designed to be the tests of our free will to become one with God.

The study of His will is not only the best way to know how to accomplish the task of our existence; it is also the act that carries with it the greatest ability to make us Godlike. Torah study is the mitzvah that can change us, elevate us, and sanctify us the most. This explains the intrinsic relationship between God, man, and Torah. It has to be that the Torah is called God's name, as we mentioned previously, because it is the instruction manual of how to connect to God. The study of Kabbalah, which is the closest thing to studying God himself, is the most potent and holy aspect of Torah study. This is the perspective to have whenever engaged in the study of Jewish mysticism; you are making your mind and soul one with your Creator.

Although the words "to become one with God" conjure up imagery of someone meditating on a mountaintop, the Torah describes the process of becoming holy as one of elevating everything in the physical realm. It is through involvement in the world that we elevate ourselves, as long as that involvement is done with God's principles. Because He designed and created humanity and their many endeavors, it is through the vehicle of human experience that we become one with Him.

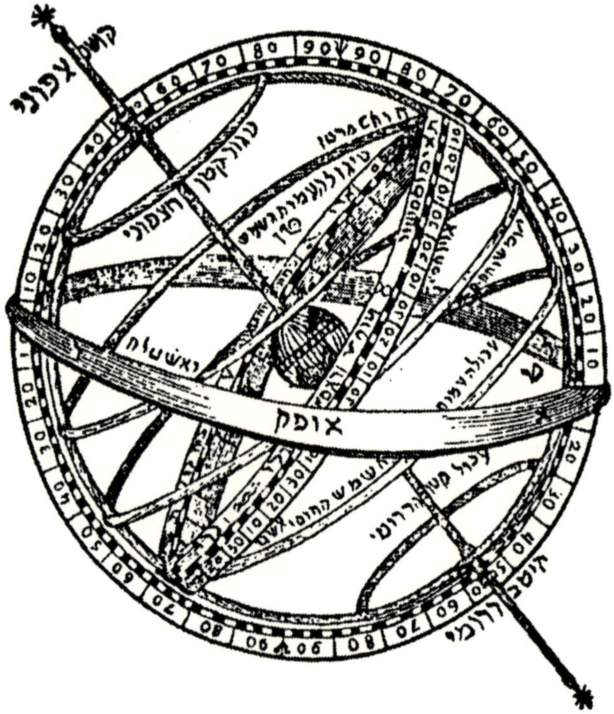
צפוני
אופק
דרומי

CHAPTER FIVE

Our World is Traveling Towards Its Destiny

"Everything has its season, and there is a time for everything under the heavens."
Ecclesiastes 3:1

Astronomers and other scientists say that life on earth has a finite amount of time to exist. There are different scenarios, but it seems inevitable there will be an end to life on Earth. There's something slightly emotionally disturbing about the thought of the end of mankind even if it's off in the future and I won't be around for it: "You mean we won't be here forever?"

Kabbalah also teaches that life as we know it won't last forever. In fact, the universe is quickly coming to the end of its journey. The Jewish calendar considers this year 5761 (at the writing of this book).[39] It is stated that the world will last 6000 years. "The universe will exist for six thousand years, another thousand in desolation, and at the end of that thousand years God will renew His world again."[40] This means we have at most 239 years left. I say "at most" because it is a Jewish belief that the messiah may come at any moment and thrust humanity into a new and different realm of being. Although anyone reading this now won't be around in 239 years to see the year 6000, this time period seems incredibly short. It is an interesting point that 239 represents a fraction of 1/25th of the total 6000 years. Kenneth Feder in *The Past in Perspective* quotes that single celled organisms appeared on earth 3.5 billion years ago. Christopher McKay of NASA Ames Research Center has a prediction that the earth will no longer be inhabitable in approximately 145 million years. If this is true, 145 million years represents the exact same fraction 1/25th of the total life span of 3.5 billion plus 145 million. Coming from two different realms, science and Kabbalah, both say we are at the very end of the cycle of life. To give an analogy, if the entire span of life is considered an hour we are in the last two and a half minutes. The finality, however, is not the main point.

    We cannot possibly fathom the intent of an infinite Being in His creation of the universe. Man's mind is finite. By definition it cannot fully grasp the Infinite. The perspective that He taught us to have is that life is here for our ultimate pleasure.[41] Man was created to come close to the infinite Being in every possible way. In order for this to take place, there needs to be two periods: a period of challenge and struggle, and a period to realize the fruits of our labor. The world we live in is the place of illusion, and striving for closeness to the Creator. It has a beginning and an end. The second stage is called "the world to come," and will last for eternity. From a spiritual point of view, in order for our reality to make sense, the world as we know it must end. If you suggest this world should continue forever, you're willing to accept all the imperfections that we live with like war, hatred, famine, etc. We are in a limited and finite world where God's existence is hidden. Is this a world that God is happy with? It can't be that a wise, loving, and infinite Being would allow this situation to continue forever.

A separate issue is the idea of the Messiah. It is a cornerstone of Jewish belief that someday a human being will bring the Jews back to the land of Israel, make a country based on the principles outlined in the Torah, and bring about an era of peace and understanding in the world.[42] This idea is mentioned many times in the Prophets, the Writings, and Talmud. For the last 1800 years, the Jews have prayed for and anticipated this person's arrival. There have been a number of potential messiahs over the years, but none have completed the task. Bar Kochba lived in Talmudic times and was a charismatic political leader that some felt was the messiah.[43] Shabbatai Tzvi, a kabbalist, lived in the 1600's and had a large following as a potential messiah.[44] Most recently Rabbi Menachem Schneerson of the Lubavitch movement was thought to be the messiah by thousands of followers.[45] Each one, for different reasons, did not complete the mission. The main reason we know they weren't the messiah is because they didn't finish the job. If any one of these people or others had or will fulfill all the criteria of the messiah, then the world as we know it will be a different place. In other words, the 6000 years that we mentioned do not have to be used up before the world is perfected. We can perfect it ourselves before that time.

It is in this context that the kabbalists are writing; and the mystical perspective on history or historical events must be viewed in this way. We cannot always see it, but there is a design in the history of man. Although we are given free will, all events that happen are part of a plan we are not privy to. Our choices cause a reaction on a spiritual level, but the entire production is being lead, directed, and influenced by the infinite Creator. It's not merely that there is an end point to life on Earth, but somehow all mankind as a unit is being perfected. Some thinkers the world over, without being privy to the kabbalistic view, have an intuitive sense of a grand master plan. A quote from the writer Lewis Thomas puts it very succinctly, "The earth holds together, its tissues cohere, and it has the look of a structure that really would make comprehensible sense if only we knew enough about it. From a little way off, photographed from the moon, it seems to be a kind of organism. Looked at over its whole time, it is plainly in the process of developing, like an enormous embryo. It is, for all its stupendous size and the numberless units and infinite variety of its life forms, coherent. Every tissue is linked for its viability to every other tissue; it gets along by symbiosis, and the invention of new modes of symbiotic coupling is a fundamental process in its embryogenesis. We have no rules for the evolution of this kind of life. We have learned a lot, and in some biomathematical detail, about the laws governing the evolution of individual species on the earth, but no Darwin has yet emerged to take account of the orderly, coordinated growth and differentiation of the whole astonishing system, much less its seemingly permanent survival. It makes an interesting problem: how do mechanisms that seem to be governed entirely by chance and randomness bring into existence new species which fit so neatly and precisely, and usefully, as though they were the cells of an organism? This is a wonderful puzzle."[46]

Of course, we know the answer to this puzzle. God. He's orchestrating this grand scheme we call history. As Rabbi Luzzatto says, "God oversees everything in the upper world and the lower world, roots and branches, and directs them constantly towards the ultimate perfection. And to this end He develops all of creation. This divides and separates each thing in creation according to its design and placement in history. Some will be pushed away from God while others will be drawn towards Him. Some will be purified through suffering, while others will be left alone. Each one gets what is fitting for it, in order for all of creation to come to its perfection."[47]

Kabbalah unites everyone who ever lived, or will live, under the banner of God's will. His goal and purpose will be achieved no matter what. Our free will is whether or not to consciously be a part of it.

אדם וחוה חץ לילית · אדם וחוה חץ לילית
סנוי וסנסנוי · וסמנגלף
שמר ד' · ויסמר ד'

CHAPTER SIX

The Spiritual World Responds to the Physical World

"Don't correct a scoffer lest he hate you; correct a wise man and he will love you."
Proverbs 9:8

Some call it—karma. Others say, "What comes around, goes around." Just as the physical world has physics, so does the spiritual. This is a rule of the spiritual world. Everything we do has an effect on the spiritual realm, and in turn the spiritual world responds.[48] If you generate love, more love will come your way. If you're tolerant of the mistakes of others, God's attribute of Justice will be more tolerant of your mistakes. It's also true that the specific type of holiness that's produced by any given commandment not only affects the person doing the act, but also the entire world. For instance, one of the commandments is to verbalize your commitment to belief in One God by saying a phrase known as the "Sh'ma"[49]—"Hear O Israel, the Lord our

God, the Lord is One."[50] When this is said, God's presence fills the entire universe to a greater degree.[51] If one person says, "Hear O Israel, the Lord our God, the Lord is One," then God's presence will fill the entire universe. When a person imitates God's attributes of mercy, the attribute of mercy is strengthened everywhere. These are all different examples of nuances of the same rule of the spiritual world; it responds in kind to man's actions. Of course we don't see it all the time, and this world is only one part of the story. The true reward and punishment is completed in the next world. There is also no way to know what the spiritual reaction may be to a particular act. Yet because the physical and the spiritual worlds are interwoven and interdependent, there has to be some response from the Heavens that affects us here on Earth.

This is what we call providence or "hashgacha" in Hebrew. Understanding how hashgacha works is part of the mystical knowledge. Kabbalah in large part is a description of how God runs the universe. It's a hidden world. We don't know all the rules. In fact sometimes the spiritual side of things seems to be in opposition to our way of looking. An interesting episode in the Talmud brings out this point. A person got very sick and his soul went up to heaven. When he recovered he was asked what he saw. "I saw an upside down world," he replied.[52] The spiritual side of life is often the opposite of what we think or feel. For example, a funeral is a sad time for the living. However, from the spiritual point of view the deceased are now going to a place of extreme pleasure and bliss. We should be happy. To drive home this point, some mystics even asked that their disciples dance on the day of the teacher's death. One famous example of this has even become somewhat of a tourist attraction in Northern Israel. Every spring people all over the world light bonfires and sing songs praising Rabbi Shimon bar Yochai, the author of the Zohar, on the anniversary of his death. On Mount Meron, near his burial spot, there are groups of visitors that camp out and the fires light up the night with festivity. What causes this odd celebration of death? The idea that in spiritual terms, Rabbi Shimon has left the world of illusion and gone back to be one with his Creator. The realm of the non-physical where God's plan is more evident is a very different world than our own.

The essence of hashgacha is the idea that everything happens for a reason. Nothing is an accident. All of one's life experiences have a spiritual purpose. God by definition is aware of and in control of every molecule of existence. If He doesn't will an event, or allow it to happen, it can't. The sages go so far as to say that since we don't have prophets to deliver God's messages, life events are the only way God can get our attention. "Problems are not necessarily a punishment for a previous transgression, rather they are a warning, sign or an indication of a potential transgression, so you don't fall into it. Problems are messengers from the Almighty sent to teach us about our faults or mistakes of the past in order for us to properly direct our future."[53] Similarly, it is a Jewish practice to analyze your deeds after a bad thing happens to you. Even a disturbing dream may be a cause for introspection.[54] This does not mean that there is a clear recognizable message from God in all the events that happen to us. We're not so astute or sensitive to always figure them out. He knows that and doesn't hold it against us. If you're looking for messages, though, you may find them. Not only that, but even if you're wrong about what area of growth you need to improve, you won't lose by correcting some other fault you have. As I heard it put from one teacher, "If you don't get diamonds, you'll still find gold."[55] Practically speaking, when trying to interpret your "sign", it's good to check out your interpretation with another person. Since interpreting Divine messages is also a challenge, the door is open to interpret an event in a self serving way. "I stubbed my toe getting out of bed. I guess God wants me to lie in bed all day and relax." Call a friend and ask what they think, just to make sure you're being honest with yourself. (I assume it goes without saying that giving unsolicited explanations of other's Divine messages may cause you to lose friends quickly.)

Although the spiritual world responds in a way that mirrors our actions, not all of our life circumstances are a reaction to something we did. Some are purely designed for our spiritual growth. God knows what situations and challenges we need to get to the next spiritual level. That's certainly the main point of all that occurs to us. For example, by having our patience tested we have the opportunity to develop more patience, which makes you more like God. Every inconvenient red light, every computer download, every wrong number is specifically designed for your internal growth in the area of patience. Even when an event we experience *is* a reaction to something we did, it comes in the context of our spiritual level and what we need for growth. The point of this rule of the spiritual realm, that it reacts to our decisions, is obviously not to be a system of reward and punishment. It can be to a partial extent, but there can't possibly be a reward in the physical world that really pays someone for a following a commandment. There's no amount of pleasure in this world to truly compensate for a spiritual achievement.

Also, we don't see righteous people getting tons of wonderful experiences and non-righteous people getting terrible circumstances. All of that is left for the next realm, the world to come. That's for eternity. The rule of spiritual interaction with us is to constantly fill our life with chances for growth and spiritual challenges that fluctuate with our own spiritual fluctuation.

With all this talk about the meaning behind every event small and large in our lives, you might get the idea that we should question all day long what's happening and why it's happening. If not done with both caution and wisdom, this might turn into a very unproductive activity. It could cause stress. It could be overwhelming. An extremely important general piece of advice to follow is this: every kabbalistic insight must be tested to see if it heightens your spiritual awareness or if it leads to confusion, or worse. Every piece of wisdom is like medicine. You have to know when and how to use it. If you start to feel some unpleasant side effects from any piece of wisdom, stop taking it unless you have consultation with a "doctor", i.e. Rabbi.

If you're striving for greatness and ethical excellence you don't necessarily need to know why you have a specific challenge. We always have the potential to rise to the occasion. If not, God won't give us that spiritual challenge. Sometimes it's better to put on blinders and merely try to be a good person in all circumstances. As it says, "You should be innocent with G-d, your Lord." (Deuteronomy 18:13) However, if you find it effective, you may learn some important insights about yourself by analyzing your life's circumstances. Nothing is an accident.

On a more global level, as mankind travels through time towards the ultimate redemption, historical events are all happening as responses from the spiritual realm.

They are designed to fit mankind's needs in terms of their spiritual growth as well as the ultimate destiny of man. Whether we see it or not, there's a reason for everything.

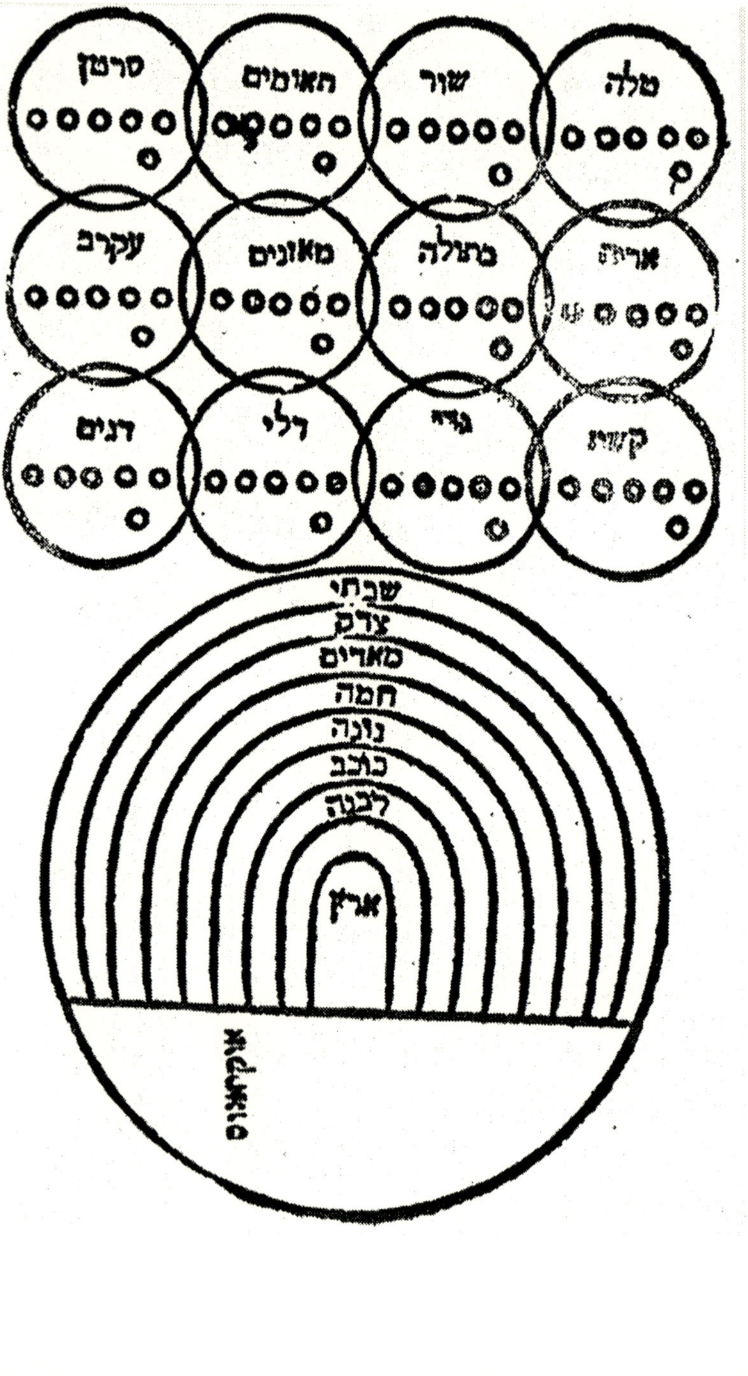

טלה
שור
תאומים
סרטן
אריה
בתולה
מאזנים
עקרב
קשת
גדי
דלי
דגים
שבתי
צדק
מאדים
חמה
נוגה
כוכב
לבנה
ארץ

CHAPTER SEVEN

All of Mankind

is Interwoven and Interdependent

> *"This is the story of the generations of Adam. On the day God created man, He made him in the likeness of God."*
> *Genesis 5:1*

Man was meant to live forever. We were originally created and designed to be a spiritual / physical unity that is connected with our infinite Creator. The first couple, Adam and Eve(*Chava*), could have been eternal.[56] This is hard to fathom given the biological reality we live with. Death is the one thing that all mortals consider inevitable. How did the plan for humanity get changed so drastically? Rabbi Moshe Chaim Luzzatto explains that the first creation made a fundamental mistake and ate the fruit that God said not to. Before they ate, they were wholly pure. By eating, they brought inside themselves a mixture of impurity. That mixture cannot be perfected unless it undergoes disintegration and then renewal. This mistake affected all of us because spiritually we are all pieces of that original man. Now every human being must die in order reach perfection. If we were to collectively rectify the blemish Adam created, we could once again reach a perfection that denies the inevitability of death.[57] Rabbi Luzzatto's explanation includes a major principle that runs through Kabbalah—that mankind, as an extension of the first man, is one. And as one unit, mankind has a collective purpose, a goal of becoming one with the Creator. If you've ever pulled on a loose thread and found yourself unraveling the fabric of a garment, then you know that sometimes one piece can also be an integral part of the whole. Mankind is a "whole" that is made up of individuals that play a crucial role in our collective purpose.

Since we are one unit, our collective purpose of connecting to the Infinite is thwarted by any one individual's transgression. Therefore we bear the negative consequences of other's mistakes. We find this expressed in the Yom Kippur[58] prayers. The formal confession, that is repeated a number of times during the prayers, is expressed in the plural: "We have betrayed. We have stolen. We have slandered, etc." Upon reading this the first time many ask, "Why am I confessing to things I haven't done?" The answer is that we are all responsible for each other's mistakes because we are one. Don't worry though; it works in our favor as well. You benefit from your fellow man's good deeds. We can elevate each other or bring each other down. How can it be fair that I'm held accountable for someone else's transgression? In the physical world we can see the influence of mob mentality or peer pressure on an individual's moral decisions and actions. The spiritual world is no different. But also, the sages tell us something very deep about the mechanics of one person's transgressions—it's not possible for one person to transgress unless the desire for that transgression lies in the heart of us all. Therefore each of us contributed in some small way to the transgression being done.

The Torah enjoins you to study all the commandments, even if you don't think you personally will violate all of them. We are also commanded to educate each other, and point out (in a kind, loving, and sensitive way) the violations or flaws that we see in each other. It's expected that we protest wrongdoing, and try to convince others of their mistakes. Commandments like, "Don't stand idly by when someone's life is in danger"[59], "You must correct your fellow man,"[60] and "You shall open your hand to your brother, to your poor and destitute in your land,"[61] underline the communal responsibility that permeates the Torah. These are not merely moral injunctions, but expressions of the spiritual reality that we are all connected. The essence of each person is his/her soul, and each soul is connected to, and a piece of, the Infinite. So all souls are connected to each other via the Infinite, and therefore they are one.

At the risk of complicating the matter, let us mention the idea of reincarnation, which we find in Judaism's mystical teachings.[62] It may seem schizophrenic but many of us may not only be the person we think we are. You may be carrying around an extra soul from someone else. You may be here for the second or third time. You may be a reincarnation of someone else, a piece of someone else, or we may share a soul with someone else who is living. It's even said that there is a piece of Moses in every Jew.[63] These aspects of reincarnation are different ways in which souls can be connected. They accentuate the interconnectedness of the spiritual realm.

Our interdependence connects us throughout our entire history, from the time of the first human until the future time of the intended perfection of all humanity. After all, the anticipation of the Messianic Era is not mainly for any individual benefit or designation of a special group, it is the hope for worldwide recognition of the oneness of the Infinite Being, as it says, "God will be King over the world. On that day God will be One and His name will be One."[64] There is a kabbalistic teaching that hints to this that says the name Adam is an acronym of the first letters of Adam, David, and Messiah ('moshiach' in Hebrew). This teaching suggests that the blueprint of the three major eras of mankind were inscribed in the first creation. More intrinsic to our discussion, though, is the name Adam itself. In English, people relate to that name merely as the first man's given name. In Hebrew, though, Adam is the word for mankind. We are all referred to as the children of Adam or merely Adam.

It just might be that when mankind realizes how tied to one another we really are, that the ultimate perfection and purpose of creation will be at hand. And then we will live forever as we were originally intended.

אין מחשבה ' תפיסא
ביה כלל

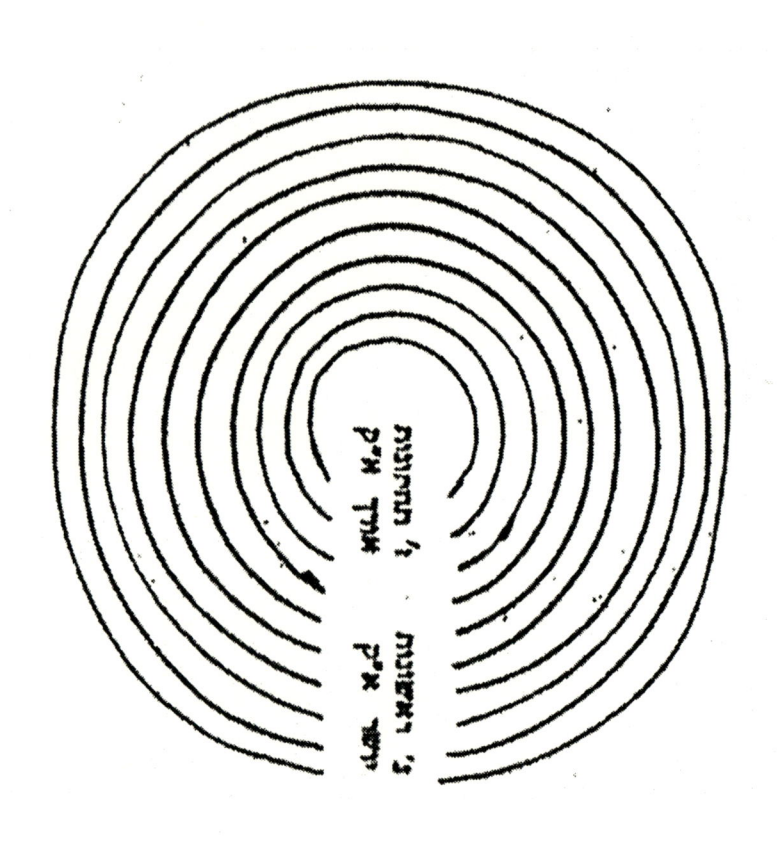

אנת הוא ' חכים
לא בחכמה ידיעא

CHAPTER EIGHT

Good and Bad Things Happen to All People

"Your rod and Your staff, they comfort me."
Psalms 23:4

We would all like to know why good happens to bad people, and bad happens to good people. It's a question that seems to always have bothered man. Moses asked the question. The entire book of Job deals with the question. Many Jewish scholars and philosophers have dealt with the issue. When the spiritual world is brought into the picture, the answer to this question become much clearer.

Our world has so much injustice, calamity, and tragedy. Anyone with even a smidgeon of a heart should cry over the tragedies written about in a single issue of a daily newspaper. However, we've become used to these daily events, and jaded. If this world is all there is then "imperfect" is too weak a word for what's been going on throughout history. The mystical view, though, is that this world is not all there is. The clock doesn't stop after death. There is a long time period that comes after this world, which would take up too many calendars to make. In fact, the length of time for the entire history of mankind will only have been a millisecond of time compared with the eternity that comes afterward. All injustices will have time to be evened out. No good deed goes unrewarded, no bad deed unrectified. Not only that but the soul in the next word is unencumbered by the fog of physicality. It becomes attached to God and will comprehend the necessity for all that it went through. In the end we will understand. We can never say there is injustice in the world, because we haven't seen the other acts of the play, we've only seen act one, scene one.

But why do the apparent injustices happen in the first place? The question implies a principle we've mentioned before, that God is not only the Creator of our reality, but He also is in control of everything in existence. Threrefore, all events that occur are either caused by His command, or at least allowed to occur by His tacit approval. If your stocks go up, He's behind it. If you stub your toe, get robbed or stabbed, He has caused or allowed it. Given the fact that in order for the world to exist as a test for man, there must be free will to do evil; we can't blame God for man's inhumanity to man. However, He still is responsible for allowing each and every injustice to happen.

Even though God is completely in touch with every nuance of existence, He's not like a father watching out for his child not to get hurt. He has a reason why He doesn't prevent apparent injustices. He created a system of how He involves Himself in our world. That system is the spiritual world. The spiritual world responds to the physical world. This means that many of the events that happen to us are a specific reaction to something we've done. It may be a benefit that comes from a good deed, or a negative consequence of a bad deed. What goes around comes around in quite a specific way. If your spiritual composition passes through one area of challenge you may even find yourself in a negative situation (from your perspective) as a result of a good deed. What it means is you've risen to a new level and you're ready for a more significant challenge. From a non-spiritual perspective a person may say, "Why is this catastrophe happening to me?" This is like a sophomore in college going into junior year saying, "but I passed my finals, why are they giving me even more complicated work to do?" When you realize fully that life is meant to be a process of spiritual growth you will accept and even welcome new challenges. After all, being given a difficult task is actually God complimenting you; He's saying, "I know you're ready for this." Your life challenges are designed for you with great precision.

How is this so? Any life situation may be a challenge or even a message from the Almighty. Some people say, "Who am I that God should trouble Himself to communicate with me, following every detail of my life?" It's no trouble for Him. He's God. He's infinite. He can communicate with every human being on the planet, every minute of the day, all at the same time with no effort whatsoever. We may not understand all the messages, but a moment's pause to reflect on a special event in your life may reap some interesting results. The very fact that you recognize God runs the world and nothing is an accident, is an elevating thought that can have powerful reverberations. The Zohar says that no blade of grass grows without an angel striking and saying, "grow."[65] Knowing that there is a meaning to everything can be calming in the face of life's many adversities. Many philosophers came to the correct conclusion that without God, everything is meaningless. What many people don't focus on, is that with God everything is meaningful.

We also know quite well that some terrible things turn out to be benefits. A woman had a miscarriage, which caused her husband and her not to go into work the next day in the World Trade Center buildings on September 11th.

Even though we know that God is somehow behind everything, we can't always figure out the "why" behind all of life's difficulties or tragedies. If we could do that, we'd be God. Some things that happen to us are recompense from previous existences, reincarnations.[66] Rabbi Luzzatto explains, "God arranged matters so that man's chances of achieving ultimate perfection should be maximized. One soul can come to this world a number of times in different bodies. This way the soul can correct in one incarnation the spiritual blemish from another incarnation, or perfect what was not perfected."[67] There's no benefit, then, to knowing why we're going through a particular difficulty. In fact, it may defeat the purpose to know the reason. It seems we're not meant to know it all. This itself is one of life's challenges, to trust the Infinite Being when we're confused by injustice.

What about when "good" things happen to bad people? What to you may seem a good thing happening to a bad person may in fact be to their detriment. The worst thing that can happen to a materialistic person is to win the lottery. The winner, of course, is ecstatic. Now, however, this person can waste even more time, and thereby lose time that could have been spent on spirituality, i.e. acquiring eternity. They can buy sixteen motorcycles, three houses, and all the other "toys" they want. Spiritually they are wallowing in the mud. People with less leisure time and money may actually be able to live a more spiritually sensitive life. Conversely, when an evil person is deprived of the ability to do evil, it is a tremendous spiritual benefit. As a wise woman I know once said to a criminal in jail, "You are very lucky they stopped you from doing more damage to your soul."

In conclusion, there are many reasons for a righteous person to suffer: it may be to test them in a specific way, like Job. It may be to give them more merit for the act, because they are enduring more difficulty in order to do the right thing, as it says, "According to the effort is the reward."[68] It may be a lesson they need to learn that will help them in the future. It may be a message from God about an area in which they need to improve. A person may get a toothache to indicate not to gossip so much. It may be atonement for past transgressions. Better in this world than the next. There may be a hidden benefit from the suffering. You may have a car accident with the man you end up marrying. All of these things can be true, and more. The perspective from the spiritual world, when the righteous suffer, is often the opposite of what one may think. For this reason many righteous individuals when faced with adversity say the following, "Whatever God does is for the good." This helps them come back to the proper perspective. If we could see the world through the eyes of Kabbalah, most injustice would come clear as true justice.

רחם תחלי דגים דלי גדי קשת עקרב מאזנים

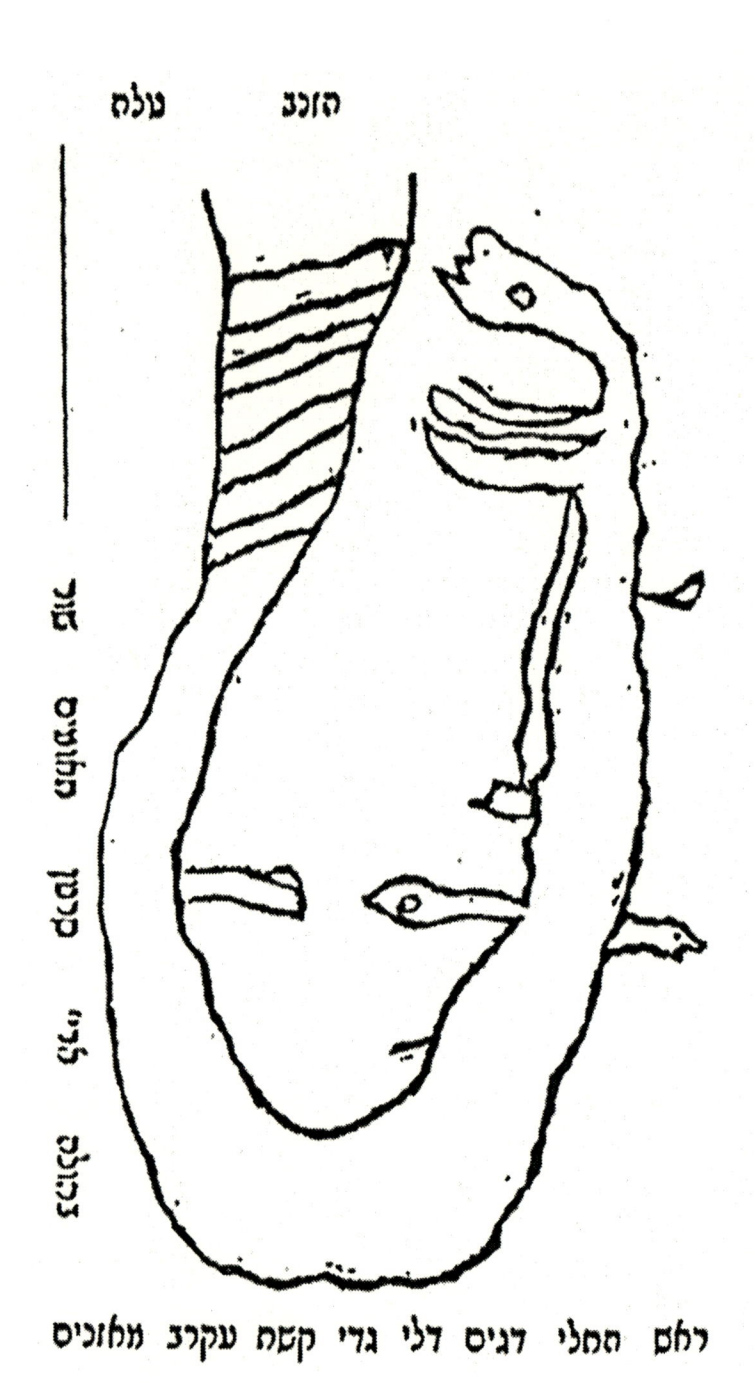

CHAPTER NINE

Life is Filled with Challenges, Lessons, and "Tikkunim"

> *"Man is born for challenging work, and sparks fly upward."*
>
> Job 5:7

Since this world is the corridor to the next, and our experience in the next world is dependent on our spiritual growth in this world, then it's clear that the purpose of life is only achieved through meaningful personal change. If you are impatient, you must become more patient. If you are quick to anger, you must become slow to anger. Everyone has work to do on themselves. If we hide from, shirk, ignore, or pass by the challenges that life offers, we are doing ourselves the most serious disservice of all. We need growth. Historically, the mystically inclined are more attuned to the reality of the next world and, therefore, our purpose here. The effect of this has been that they have traditionally taken a keener interest in personal reflection, contemplation, and change. Sometimes they went to great lengths in order to affect these changes. They would leave home and family to travel and endure hardships. They would sleep on the floor and eat bread and water to nullify the need for physical desire. Extreme behavior like this is not necessary, but some attempt to mold ourselves certainly is. You can affect your own changes. You can mold and shape your own spiritual reality. If a person will do the work on him/herself, there is less need for challenges to be brought on a person from above. If we don't grow on our own, we are sent challenges to cause us to grow.

The entire book of Job shows us an example of a challenge that replaced someone's personal growth. In the beginning of the book God indicates to the prosecuting angel that Job is a very righteous person. The angel replies that his righteousness is due to the many blessings God has bestowed upon him. Give him pain and suffering and his righteousness will cease. "The Satan answered God and said, 'Is it for nothing that Job fears God? Have You not set a protective wall about him, about his household, and about everything he owns from all around? You have blessed his work, and his flock has spread throughout the land. But send forth Your hand and touch all that he has, he will curse You to Your face.'"[69] The angel is pointing out that Job's personality has not been challenged with suffering. Therefore he is tested in order for him to have the chance to reach a higher level of righteousness. If he can love God through difficulties, he is an even greater person. Had Job challenged himself and worked on raising his connection with God above and beyond appreciation for his blessings, he wouldn't have needed to be tested. We can attempt to elevate ourselves, or we can have circumstances thrust upon us from the spiritual realm that elevate us through challenge. Either way is a benefit for us.

Not all challenges are the pain and suffering of Job, of course. They can be any moral dilemma, minor annoyance, or crossroads you face. Most of the points of growth we have are all in the same range of moral choices and therefore do not affect us in a significant way. You may have office workers who annoy you, children who test your patience, and the battle of controlling your eating habits. This is your natural realm of tests. Once in a while we face a major dilemma that causes us to tap into a much deeper part of ourselves. At that time you may feel like the movie caricature with a devil on one shoulder and an angel on the other each trying to convince you which way to go. Someone's spouse flirts with you, a Brinks truck leaves a bag of money on the curb near you, or a loved one passes away. It is that type of experience that changes the direction of your life, and, based on how you handle the test, brings about a very different set of consequences from the spiritual realm. That major challenge can move you up or down a floor in the apartment building of spiritual challenges. The spiritual responds to the physical and sets up new and different challenges and lessons based on your decisions. That major dilemma is also an indication of the specific area you really need to grow in. A challenge is not an indication you are bad, rather it is an indication you are able to be even better, as it says in Psalms 11:5, "God tests the righteous."

Somewhat separate from the many challenges we face is a specific challenge that is our main test in life. This major test affects us and humanity in a defined way, which was constructed by God. This is known as a "tikkun." Litaken in Hebrew means "to fix." Your tikkun is that one spiritual blemish that you are created with, that represents your particular contribution to the tikkun of all mankind. We are not necessarily meant to know what that tikkun is. You may, however, be in touch with yourself enough to get a general idea. They say the prophets could tell you what your individual tikkun was. Rabbi Isaac Luria, the famous sixteenth century kabbalist, was known to have been able to do this. There may even be kabbalists alive today who have this ability. However, there's a reason why God does or does not let us know our personal test. Everything around us, though, is a part of that tikkun. Your parents, your children, and your neighbors are all part of your tikkun. Even your spouse is part of your tikkun. If after you're married for a while you feel like everything about her/him is great except for 'one thing', God may have planted that one thing there. Not for your spouse, but for you to have the challenge of dealing with that conflict.

Keeping all this in mind, what may appear to you as the biggest problem of your life, may in fact be your greatest spiritual benefit. When you deal with that challenge you may be perfecting your most important character trait. This is an important, insightful, and peaceful way of looking at life in the face of adversity. The calmness that this perspective will give you will also give you a much greater chance of passing that test.

Kabbalists throughout the ages took a very serious attitude towards self-growth. They looked at every difficulty in life as a challenge, every challenge as a lesson, and every lesson as a tikkun. This is all of life. No matter how great you are, life will give you challenges according to your stature. Not a single one of the great sages, prophets, and holy ones of Israel lived without challenges. The kabbalists also recognized that the true path to enlightenment is dependent more upon one's character than upon one's access to the mystical wisdom, or one's desire to know that wisdom. Devorah reached the highest spiritual level possible, prophecy, because of her character. As it says in Tana D'bei Eliahu, "I testify before the heavens and the earth, whether someone is Jewish or not, man or woman, slave or maidservant, everything is dependent upon deed. That's what causes the Divine spirit to rest on someone. Devorah said to her husband, 'I will make wicks, and you will take them to the Temple in Jerusalem.'"[70] Devorah was not expected to do such a righteous act. She was going beyond the call of duty in order to gain a spiritual merit. Because of her devotion, God bestowed enlightenment on her. So we see that character development is what leads to a greater mystical experience. We need challenges as messages from God to tell us what to work on. We need challenges to force us to grow. We need challenges to fulfill our mission in life.

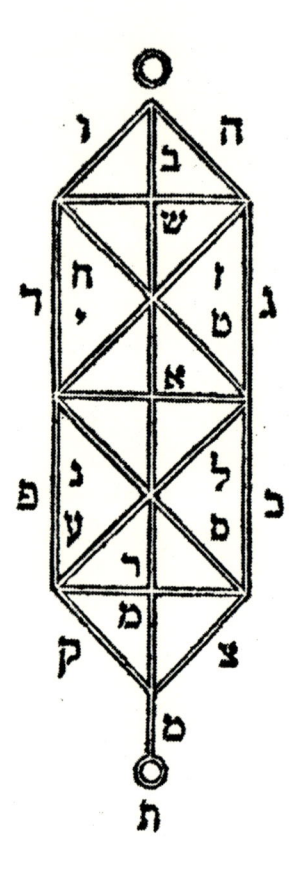

CHAPTER TEN

The Letters of the Hebrew Alphabet are the Building Blocks of Creation

> *"Twenty and two foundational letters: He engraved them in voice, carved them in wind, and set them in the mouth."*
> *Sefer Yetzira 2:3*

God's existence is very far removed from anything we can comprehend. He is immanent and part of everything we know; yet we cannot know Him. To ponder Him confounds the mind. As He said to Moses, "No man can see me and live." (Exodus 33:20) Why can we not "see" God? Because a human being, being hindered by the barrier of physicality, is not capable of grasping God. Like a bright light can be blinding, so is God's presence to a mortal. However, when someone dies and the soul is detached from the body, then he can see God.

Although everything is part of God, including us, in between our existence and God's true essence are levels and layers of worlds, universes, and spiritual entities. God created and designed all of these things. The study and understanding of these forces and realities are a large part of kabbalistic thought. There are upper realms and lower realms all in an intricately entwined matrix-type design linking our realm of reality to worlds above which ascend to a reality much closer to God's essence. Since these realms are created as form without matter, they do not have spatial relationships. Hence, as soon as we try to picture these realms and levels we are distorting our understanding. This causes quite an obstacle for many to a true understanding of the spiritual world. Many kabbalistic works have diagrams or visual configurations of spiritual entities. It's very important to be clear that as in Geometry, a circle is a concept not a reality, so too these diagrams don't represent any type of physicality, but rather a conceptual view of spirituality.

To aid our ability to understand the spiritual side, God gave hints and clues in the physical realm, and in the Torah. The Hebrew language is the foundation of the Torah, and the alphabet is the backbone of the language. Other languages may have evolved organically, or developed from one language mixing with another. Hebrew was something that was formed by an Infinite Being and has intrinsic meaning and holiness. The Torah was dictated to Moses by God to be written in Hebrew. God created the Hebrew language, which is what everyone spoke until the Tower of Babel incident.[71] At that point, God caused a dispersion of the nations and the creation of their respective languages.[72] Each Hebrew letter is a symbol of a spiritual reality that God created. Each letter has a name and an importance all its own. For example, the letter Vav is the sixth letter of the aleph-bet. The word "vav" means a hook. The letter also functions grammatically as a hook as it is often used to be the word "and." Visually, the letter looks like a hook, too. There is importance placed on the way each letter is pronounced as it emanates from a different part of the mouth.[73] The letters that come from the same place in the mouth have a conceptual similarity as well. Each letter also represents a number and that number has significance in Jewish thought. As Vav is the sixth letter, it stands for the number six. Therefore this letter will have a special relationship with the six directions (N, S, E, W, up, and down), the six days of creation, the six permutations of the letters of God's name[74], and other groups of six in the mystical writings. Each word in Hebrew is usually made up of several letters, and there are different ways of calculating the numerical significance of each word or sentence. The study of the numerical significance of letters, words, sentences, etc. in Judaism is called Gematria. Numerical significance is a concept that runs throughout the mystical literature. One example of this occurs in Genesis 37:4. It says, " . . . they could not speak to him peaceably." The brothers of Joseph were jealous of him and their speech reflected this. The word "peaceably" has the numerical value of 400. This alludes to the prophecy that Israel would be enslaved for 400 years in Egypt.[75] Why does this particular sentence allude to the Egyptian exile? Because the strife between the brothers and Joseph was considered a partial cause of the eventual exile of the Jews.[76] All throughout the Torah there are words whose numerical values hint to deeper insights.

There are twenty-two letters of the aleph-bet, which are divided into three groups by the kabbalists: A group of three that are symbolic of the primordial elements with which God created physicality: air, water, and fire. A group of seven that are symbolic of the seven main celestial bodies: Sun, Moon, Mars, Mercury, Jupiter, Venus, and Saturn. These in turn have a connection with the seven days of the week. Each body influences a different day. The sun influences Sunday, the moon Monday, etc. And a last group of twelve that are symbolic of the twelve signs of the zodiac, and the twelve months, which have a spiritual connection to the twelve tribes of Jacob.

Each of these three groups of letters symbolizes a function in the world aside from its representation of a higher reality. The stars and planets are conduits for the spiritual influences from above. The first two groups of three and seven can be combined to form a group of ten. This group is the precursor to the ten statements of creation, the ten plagues in Egypt, and the Ten Commandments. Ten is a unit. It represents completeness. God hid the knowledge of how the spiritual world is structured; yet at the same time He revealed it to us through the stars, planets, and the alphabet. The Torah also hints to much of the mystical side of the universe. If you are sensitive to the words and looking for spiritual insights you will find them in the Torah, the Prophets, the Writings, and also the Siddur.

Understand that this group of ten is an essential theme in Kabbalah. It expresses ten qualities of Godliness that we find in the world. These ten qualities are known as the Sefirot, and they exist as the backbone of the spiritual realm that exists somehow between God's essence and our reality.

What is the purpose of the knowledge of these sefirot or any of the other aspects of Kabbalah? All of existence is here for us to come closer to God. Every commandment is an opportunity for a connection to God, and every piece of Torah knowledge binds you to God. It's His book, and His instructions. This is the purpose of the Torah and the commandments. The study of Kabbalah in particular describes how God runs the universe, which is a much more powerful and more revealing glimpse of God's actual self, so to speak. We can never, as we've said, really know God while we are in the body. Kabbalah, however, gives us the greatest possibility of closeness. For this reason, Kabbalah in traditional sources is called "Chochmas Elokus" which means "The knowledge of Godliness". One who studies Kabbalah without wanting to understand and get closer to the Almighty is like reading a book on advanced geometry because you like the looks of the diagrams. You're missing the point. If you separate Kabbalah from its source then you no longer have Kabbalah. You have something else. One must be involved in some way with Torah study and mitzvah observance in order to really ever know Kabbalah.

There are many other aspects to the Hebrew letters and language. The first step in Torah study and/or the study of Kabbalah lies within this approach. Given the fact that God began with the creation of the Hebrew language, it would seem that is the logical place to start. Study Hebrew and you are opening up all the avenues of wisdom that God has to pour out to you.

IN CONCLUSION

The ideas presented in this book are just the beginning of the beginning. Without them, it is impossible to truly understand anything about Kabbalah. Yet they are still only the foundation on which to build your knowledge. The spiritual world is infinite and the study of that world never ending. However, when we find truth, we see it was always inside us. Finding that world is like finding a long lost brother coming back home. It's like finding a part of yourself you never knew. The more you delve, the more you find yourself.

NOTES

1. The Talmud is sixty volumes of law, custom, ethical principles and explanations of Biblical verses. It is the main focus of study for scholars in traditional Judaism.
2. Amos is the second of the twelve later prophets. It says in 8:11 "Behold, days are coming, says the Lord, God, and I will send a famine in the land, not a famine for bread, and not a thirst for water, but rather to hear the words of God."
3. There is a tradition that mystical information was given to Adam some two thousand years before the revelation on Mt. Sinai, and therefore may have been handed down and been possessed by other religions or peoples besides the Jews.
4. Jewish Law is called "Halachah" in Hebrew
5. An 18th Century kabbalist. See appendix
6. After the Men of the Great Assembly the chain of tradition was kept alive by sages known as Tannaim(teachers). They included such sages as Hillel and Rabbi Akiva. The sages that followed them who lived in the Talmudic period(until 500 C.E.) were called Amoraim(discussers). The sages who followed them, until 1000 C.E., were known as the Geonim(great ones). Saadya Gaon and Rav Hai Gaon

were noted sages from that period. The sages who followed them, until 1500 C.E. were known as the Rishonim(first ones) and included Maimonides, Nachmanides, and Rashi, to name a few. All of the sages since that time are called Acharonim(later ones), and continue to carry on the unbroken chain of transmission.

7   See Ethics of Our Fathers 1:1
8   The Mishna is the original codification by Rabbi Yehuda HaNasi of the Oral Law. It was written down in 188 c.e.
9   Mishna Chagiga 2:1
10 Commentary Tiferes Israel on the Mishna
11 i.e. Became a heretic
12 Tractate Chagiga page 14b
13 The word for orchard in Hebrew is "pardes" which is an acronym for the four words, "pshat," "remez," "drush," and "sod." They are the four levels of understanding through which the Torah can be understood: 1- the simple meaning, 2 - a hint, 3 - a derivation, and 4 - a secret. Although "orchard" refers to all levels of understanding, it is used specifically to refer to the mystical teachings.
14 The Zohar is the most famous compendium of Kabbalah. It is attributed to Rabbi Shimon bar Yochai from the 2nd Century c.e. Most of the study of Kabbalah throughout the ages has been based on this book.
15 Igeres HaKodesh Chapter 26
16 Sefer Deah p.76 "...Parshas VaYera p.117 'and in the 600th year of the 6th millennium the gates of wisdom will be opened from above and wellsprings from below, and the world will begin to prepare itself for the 7th millennium, like a man who prepares

himself Friday afternoon for the Sabbath. The hint to this is in Genesis 7:11, "In the six hundredth year of Noah's life...all the fountains of the great deep burst forth.'" And when the Zohar says 'will be opened' it means that permission is given to all who desire to cling to God and delve into Kabbalah with the proper intention. Anyone who looks into this matter will see and realize that this wasn't the case before 5600. At that time Kabbalah was hidden and secret, only the few worthy individuals had access. This I heard in the name of the wise and righteous Rabbi Yisroel Salanter."

17 Rabbi Noah Weinberg
18 Exodus 33:12-20
19 See Chapter One for example
20 Psalms 25:14
21 Tractate Niddah 30b
22 Tractate Sanhedrin 37a
23 Of course He is beyond the universe as well.
24 Genesis 1:26
25 Zohar Yitro 75b
26 Path of the Just, Chapter One
27 Gate 4, Chapter 11
28 Way of God 1:2:5
29 Parshas Acharey 72b
30 Yad HaChazakah, Foundations of Torah 2:10
31 Deuteronomy 30:11
32 Talmud, Tractate Makkos 24a
33 See also Deuteronomy 10:20, 13:5, 28:9
34 Way of God, Luzzatto 1:2
35 Path of the Just Chapter 1
36 The Complete Artscroll Siddur page 59
37 Genesis 32:5, Rashi commentary
38 Genesis 1:26

39. This is not necessarily a negation of the present scientific viewpoint that the universe is billions of years old. This is subject addressed by other authors more qualified in the scientific area. Read Genesis and the Big Bang, or The Science of God, by Dr. Gerald Schroeder.
40. Talmud Tractate Sandhedrin 97a
41. Path of the Just, Chapter 1
42. #12 of Maimonides' Thirteen Principles of Jewish Belief
43. Talmud Tractate Sanhedrin 93b
44. Although some historians will include Jesus as a potential messiah, he was never considered a potential messiah by the Jews.
45. Out of the three "messiahs" mentioned, only Rabbi Schneerson died with a positive reputation.
46. The Medusa and the Snail
47. The Way of God, 2:5:5
48. Talmud Tractate Sota 8b, Tractate Sanhedrin 90a
49. Book of Mitzvah Education (Sefer HaChinuch) Mitzvah #420
50. Deuteronomy 6:4
51. Way of God 4:4:3
52. Tractate Bava Basra 10b
53. Toras Avraham by Rabbi Avraham Grodzensky, Section title "Yisurim" page 28
54. Code of Jewish Law, Orech Chaim 220
55. Rabbi Noah Orlowek
56. See commentaries to Genesis 2:17
57. Way of God 1:3
58. The Day of Atonement, a Biblical fast day that occurs each year in the fall
59. Leviticus 19:16
60. Leviticus 19:17

61	Deuteronomy 15:11
62	Rabbi Tzaddok HaCohen, Tzidkas HaTzaddik, Section Nine; Rabbi Luzzatto, Way of God 2:3:10
63	Tanya Chapters 42, 44
64	Zechariah 14:9
65	Zohar 1:34
66	This explains, as well, why young children may suffer or die.
67	The Way of God 2:3:10
68	Ethics of Our Fathers 5:26
69	Job 1:9-11
70	Chapter 9, Tana D'Bei Eliahu is a collection of teachings from Elijah the prophet
71	Commentary by Rashi to Genesis 11:1
72	Genesis 11:9
73	The five places that pronounce the letters are throat, palette, tongue, teeth, and lips. Each letter is pronounced mainly from one of these places. For example, the letter "tet" mainly comes from the teeth.
74	God's primary name in Hebrew is a four-letter name. One letter is repeated in the name, so the name is really comprised of three different letters. The six permutations of those letters have special significance in Kabbalah.
75	See Genesis 15:13
76	Commentary Baal Haturim on Genesis 37:4

INDEX

Abraham 32, 37
Act of Creation, "maaseh beraishis" 16, 19
Act of the Chariot, "maaseh merkavah" 16, 17, 19
Adam 55, 56, 58
afterlife 21
angel(s) 30, 63, 68
Bar Kochba 43
Bible 20, 23, 24, 30, 36
calendar 41
challenges 50, 63, 64, 67-71
chance 44
commandment(s) 20, 30, 36-38, 47, 51, 76, 77
converts 30
Darwin, Charles 44
death 48, 49, 55, 56
design in the universe 31, 44, 62
Devorah 71
enlightenment 71
evolution 44
Ezekiel 21
free will 38, 39, 44, 45, 62

gematria 75
gentile 29, 30
God
  name of 24, 31, 75
  presence of 26, 30, 32, 37, 38, 48, 73
  will of 26, 30-32, 37, 39, 45, 49
Hebrew 74-77
history 32, 44, 45, 96
humility 37
infinite 20, 24, 25, 36-38, 42-44, 55, 57, 58, 63
injustice 61, 62, 64, 65
Israel
  land of 43, 49
  people of 29, 30, 32
Jacob 32, 76
Job 61, 65, 68, 69
karma 47
King David 58
Maimonides 33
magic 15
matzah 37, 38
meditation 15, 18, 95
medrash 15, 30

merkavah 17, 19
messiah 21, 42, 43, 58,
Mishna 16, 30, 82, 101
mitzvah 19, 37, 39, 77, 100
Moses 15, 16, 20, 32, 58, 61, 73
Mt. Sinai 29, 37, 95
Oral Law 12, 15, 16, 18, 20, 30, 91
orchard, "Pardes" 18, 82
Patriarchs, forefathers 32, 37
Passover 37
physicality 16, 25, 27, 38, 62, 73
pleasure 36, 42, 48
Prophets 49, 70, 95
providence 48, 49
purpose of life 17, 32, 36, 56, 67
Rabbi Akiva 17, 18, 81, 96
Rabbi Isaac Luria, Ari 19, 70, 97
Rabbi Menachem Mendel Schneerson 43
Rabbi Shimon bar Yochai 19, 49, 96
Rabbi Shneur Zalman of Liadi 19, 93
randomness 44
reincarnation 57, 58, 64, 100
resurrection of the dead 21
revelation 29-31, 37, 95
reward and punishment 29, 48, 50, 62
righteous gentile 29
Satan 68
science 42
sefirot 76, 101
Shabbatai Tzvi 43
signs 49
soul 18, 20, 25, 26, 29, 30, 37, 57, 62, 73
spirituality 12, 38, 74
suffering 45, 65, 68
superstitions 16
Talmud 12, 15, 17, 30, 43, 81, 92, 96, 101
Ten Commandments 76
tikkun 67-71, 101
Torah 20, 25, 29-32, 38, 39, 74, 77, 101
Tower of Babel 74
transgression 24, 49, 56, 57, 65
universe 17, 24-26, 31, 32, 38, 48
world to come 30, 37, 42, 48, 51, 67
Writings 12, 15, 18, 30, 43, 76
Written Law 15, 20
Yom Kippur 56
Zohar 19, 82, 91, 102
zodiac 76

BIBLICAL SOURCES QUOTED

Source		Page
Genesis	1:26	26, 38
	5:1	55
	7:11	83
	37:4	75
Exodus	33:20	31, 73
Leviticus	19:1, 2	35
	19:16	57
	19:17	57
Deuteronomy	6:4	48
	10:12	36
	11:22	36
	15:11	57
	18:13	51
	30:11	36

Amos	8:11	81
Zechariah	14:9	29, 58
Psalms	8:4-6	23
	11:5	69
	23:4	61
	25:14	21
	101:7	17
	116:15	18
Proverbs	3:32	15
	9:8	47
	25:16	18
Job	1:9-11	68
	5:7	67
Ecclesiastes	3:1	41

CLASSICAL SOURCES OF THE ORAL TRADITION QUOTED IN "MAP OF THE UNIVERSE"

Mishna Tractate Chagigah—the entire Mishna is the backbone of the oral tradition. It was handed down from God to Moses and then from teacher to student orally. Eventually it was written down and codified in the early part of the common era.

Mishna Tractate Pirkey Avot

Zohar—attributed to the Talmudic sage Rabbi Shimon bar Yochai, it was kept oral and secret until a written copy was revealed in the 1500's.

Tana D'Bei Eliahu—a medrashic compilation attributed to Elijah the Prophet

Sefer Yetzira—a terse kabbalistic treatise attributed to Abraham which is known to have been studied and then used to perform acts of creating live beings.

Siddur—the standard traditional prayerbook originally compiled in Talmudic times.

Talmud Tractates: Chagigah
                    Sotah
                    Bava Basra
                    Sandhedrin
                    Makos

The Talmud elucidates and analyzes the Mishna. It was compiled over years and completed in the late 300's A.C.E.

The following are works by individual sages and mystics, arranged chronologically:

Yad HaChazakah or Mishna Torah—Maimonides' code of Jewish Law—Maimonides was a great Spanish sage, philosopher, and doctor who lived in the 1100's.

Sefer HaChinuch (Book of Education)—A book that articulates every one of the 613 commandments in the Bible, with a short description, a possible deeper reason for the commandment and a few of the laws. Attributed to Aharon HaLevi, a sage from the late 1200's.

Rashi—acronym for Rabbi Shlomo Yitzchaki, an 11th century French rabbi who wrote the most used and most authoritative commentary to the Bible and the Talmud.

Baal HaTurim—A commentary on the Bible written by Rabbi Yaakov ben HaRosh who lived in the late 1200's and early 1300's. This commentary deals with gematria, the system of looking at the Hebrew letters of a text as a number. (see glossary of Hebrew terms)

Code of Jewish Law known as the Shulchan Aruch—a compendium of all the known laws at the time of Rabbi Yosef Karo, the author, who wrote down the majority opinion (more or less) of the earlier sages who had compiled the laws of Judaism. He lived in the 1500's.

The Way of God—a book by Rabbi Moshe Chaim Luzzatto, an Italian sage and kabbalist who lived in the early 1700's, that describes logically and succinctly the structure and purpose of everything existence.

Path of the Just—a book by the same author that gives a system of spiritual growth that leads to prophecy.

Tanya—a book by the Chassidic master Rabbi Shneur Zalman of Liadi who lived in the late 1700's. The work weaves together character development and mystical ideas. He was the founder of the Lubavitch branch of Chassidim.

Iggeres HaKodesh—a work by the same author offering spiritual guidance and encouragement.

Nefesh HaChaim—a work by Rabbi Chaim Voloszhin who lived in the late 1700's early 1800's, that explains the mystical understanding of man's being created "in the image of God."

Tiferes Yisrael—a commentary on the Mishna, written by Rabbi Yisroel Lipshitz who lived in the 1800's.

Toras Avraham—an ethical/philosophical work by Rabbi Avrohom Grodzensky who lived in the late 1800's early 1900's.

Sefer Deah—one volume of a two volume work by Rabbi Shlomo Elyashev, known as Leshem Shevo Ve'achlama, published at the beginning of the 1900's.

BIOGRAPHICAL NOTES ON WELL KNOWN KABBALISTS

It should be noted that many wise and holy people were never labeled as a kabbalist or a mystic, yet they were very well versed in the mystical tradition. Also, some holy people keep their identity a secret and the world never knows their spiritual accomplishments.

Although some of the mystical information taught as Kabbalah is attributed to Adam and Abraham, and there was a tradition that was handed down from the time of Adam until the time of Abraham, the main body of information is that which came from the revelation on Mt. Sinai. God taught Moses the mystical tradition or Kabbalah along with the rest of the teachings of Judaism. It was kept as part of the Oral Tradition and never extensively written down.

Some people make the mistake of thinking only Ezekiel amongst the prophets was a mystic because of the obvious mystical allusions in his book of prophecy. But it's clear that all the prophets engaged in mystical meditation in order to open themselves up to prophecy.

During the Talmudic Era, from approximately 100 B.C.E. until 500 C.E., there were many sages who were mystically inclined. Amongst those more well known for these inclinations were Rabbi Yochanan ben Zakkai, Rabbi Yonason ben Uziel, Rabbi Akiva, Rabbi Chananya ben Chanikai, Rabbi Nechunia ben Hakaneh, and most notably Rabbi Shimon bar Yochai, the author of the Zohar.

Throughout history there have been so many great people well versed in Kabbalah that it would take a book just to give a brief biography on them all. There are many important people I have to leave out since this isn't the format to give everyone room. I am only listing some of the sages who left a particular mark on the history of Kabbalah and therefore a person beginning a serious study of the subject would benefit from knowing them. But these are not the only or even the most important ones.

Rabbi Avraham Ibn Ezra (1089-1164) Born in Spain. Most noted for his grammatical commentary on the Holy Writings. He delved extensively into Jewish Astrology.

Rabbi Moshe ben Nachman, Nachmanides, Ramban (1194-1270) Born in Spain and died in the Holy Land. Wrote first openly mystical commentary on the Bible.

Rabbi Avraham Abulafia (1240-1291) Wrote extensively on topics of meditation. One of the most influential, colorful, and controversial of all the kabbalists. Tried to convert the Pope in 1279.

Rabbi Yosef Gikatalia (1248-1305) A student of Abulafia who wrote, among many other books, an extremely influential book called Shaarey Orah, "Gates of Light" on the Sefirot (Ten Emanations).

Rabbi Don Yitzchak Abarbanel (1437-1508) A very prominent, wealthy, sage who lived in Portugal, Spain, and Italy. He was finance minister to King Ferdinand and Queen Isabella and was instrumental in helping Columbus. He left willingly during the time of the expulsion. He authored a number of books on the subject of the messiah.

Rabbi Yosef Caro (1488-1575) Most known as the author of the Code of Jewish Law which became the compendium of Jewish Law agreed upon by all Jews. He also wrote a book based on his conversations with an angel who visited him regularly.

Rabbi Moshe Cordevero (1522-1570) A leader of the Safed, Israel community of kabbalists. He made a major impact on the study of Kabbalah by clarifying and systematizing the ideas found in the Zohar.

Rabbi Yehuda Loewe, the Maharal (1525-1609) Wrote many kabbalistic/philosophical works with originality and creativity. He is most famous for the legend of his creating a golem, a fake human.

Rabbi Yitzchak Luria, the Holy Ari (1534-1572) After Rabbi Shimon bar Yochai and his Zohar, the Ari is probably the most influential of all the kabbalists. His explanation of the information in the Zohar became the accepted understanding. Almost all works of Kabbalah since then clarify and discuss the Ari's ideas.

Rabbi Chaim Vital (1543-1620) The main student of the Ari who wrote down his master's teachings for everyone to study.

Baal Shem Tov (1698-1760) The founder of the movement known as the Chassidim. He introduced a new way of incorporating kabbalistic ideas into daily living and a way of life. Most of the leaders of the groups of this movement were great kabbalists. (The name "Baal Shem" was a common name for a leader of a kabbalistic circle.)

Rabbi Moshe Chaim Luzzatto (1707-1747) A young controversial genius who wrote a number of classics on a variety of topics including language, logic, and ethics, from a kabbalistic viewpoint. One of the most multitalented sages who ever lived.

Rabbi Eliahu of Vilna, the Vilna Gaon (1720-1797) Wrote on all areas of Torah. Was known to be of greater stature in knowledge and comprehension than everyone else including sages from some previous generations.

Chacham Yosef Chaim (1832-1904) Lived in Baghdad. Wrote a number of works that became the standard for Sephardic Jews.

This is only a partial list of some of the more prominent kabbalists throughout the history of Kabbalah. Some were well integrated into society; others were reclusive. Some were mystical bordering on self-proclaimed prophecy; others were more grounded, rational and logical. There is no one personality of a kabbalist.

GLOSSARY OF HEBREW TERMS

Ain Sof—lit. without end, One way the kabbalists refer to God.

Ben—son of, Throughout Jewish history sages have often been known by their first name and the name of their father, e.g. Eliezer ben Hyrkanos is Eliezer the son of Hyrkanos.

Chacham (f. chachama)—a sage

Chassidim—lit. pious ones, Followers of a movement within traditional Judaism that started in the 1700's. The sages that lead the branches of this movement have commonly spoken more openly about kabbalistic topics than the sages not associated with this movement.

Chochmas Elokus—lit. wisdom of Godliness, Another way of referring to the study of Kabbalah.

Dveykus—lit. clinging, a feeling of being one with God.

Gematria—a branch of kabbalistic study that looks at letters or words in Scripture as numbers. This area of study includes many systems by which to count the number associated with a particular word and a number of ways to conclude what the Bible may be hinting to based on numerical significance.

Gilgul—reincarnation.

Hashgacha—lit. oversee, How God oversees His creation.

Hisbodedus—seclusion or meditation

Hisbonenus—contemplation

Kabbalah—lit. that which is received, The mysticism of Judaism.

Kavanah—concentration

Klipos—lit. shells, In the spiritual realm, a type of covering that act as a barrier to deeper spirituality.

Maaseh Beraishis—lit. act of creation, An area of Kabbalah that deals with the creation of the universe and the primordial spiritual forces.

Maaseh Merkava—lit. act of the chariot, An area of Kabbalah that deals with sanctifying oneself, and meditation.

Malach—angel.

Mazal—constellation (fortune).

Medrash—lit. exposition, A section of the Oral Tradition that explains many verses of scripture.

Mekubal—lit. one who receives, A person who is well versed in Kabbalah.

Mikva—a ritual pool used for emersion by people who want to be cleansed of different types of spiritual impurity.

Mishna—lit. teaching, Sixty volumes of statements that form the backbone of the Oral Tradition God gave to Moses.

Misnagdim—lit. opposers, People who opposed the movement of the Chassidim.

Mitzvah—commandment, or a good deed.

Moshiach—lit. anointed one, Usually refers to the messiah.

Navi—prophet.

Nefesh, Neshama, Ruach,—all names for the soul.

Olam—world, universe or realm.

Olamot—lit. worlds, A major topic of Kabbalah is the four worlds that make up reality: The world of physicality, The world of angels, The world of spiritual forces, and the world of Godliness.

Pardes—lit. orchard, A euphemism in Kabbalah for advanced meditation.

Rabbi—title given to one qualified to render decisions in Jewish Law. Can be in a position of leadership or teaching.

Ruach HaKodesh—lit. spirit of holiness, A type of Divine inspiration on a lower level than prophecy.

Sefer—book.

Sefer Yetzirah—lit. book of creation, An ancient Kabbalistic work attributed to Abraham.

Sefirot—lit. emanations, Ten Divine qualities that are an underlying structure in the universe, and a major topic in Kabbalah.

Sh'ma—lit. listen, A prayer said twice a day affirming one's conviction in Monotheism.

Talmud—lit. study, A compendium of the analysis of the Mishna by the early sages of that time period. Includes laws, debates, anecdotes, and mystical allusions.

Tikkun—lit. fix, a specific test that can fix a significant spiritual blemish in a person.

Torah—lit. instruction, Can refer to the five books of Moses, or any or all of the wisdom God taught the Jews.

Tazddik (f. tzadeykus)—a righteous individual

Tzimtzum—lit constrict, major concept in Kabbalah that discusses the act of God's hiding Himself, so to speak, in order to allow mankind to have free will.

Yichudim—lit. unifications, A meditative device used by the kabbalists that employs mental imaging of Divine names.

Zohar—lit. brightness, A large work that is the basis for most of the Kabbalah that is studied today.

More of Rabbi Weiman's articles on a variety of topics such as dreams, reincarnation, magic, Satan, and superstition can be found at his website *www.kabbalahclub.com*

To receive monthly articles via email or to ask Rabbi Weiman a question, contact *Mweiman@aish.com*

ABOUT THE AUTHOR

Rabbi Max Weiman has studied Judaism in Israel and the U.S. since 1983. He spent time in a variety of traditional yeshivot, and received ordination from the Chief Rabbi of Jerusalem through Yeshivat Aish HaTorah in 1992. At that point he began teaching for Aish, an international Jewish education movement.

In 1999 he formed the Kabbalah Club and has been teaching via classes, email, newspaper articles, and a website *www.kabbalahclub.com*.

His articles have appeared in the Jewish Press, Intermountain Jewish News, St. Louis Jewish Light, Pathfinder, Bulletin of the Astrological Association of St. Louis, and Today's Astrologer and various websites.

Rabbi Weiman lives in St. Louis, Missouri with his wife, Chava, and their six children.

Dedicated in the memory of

Jacob Singer

By

Bob Orell and Linda Lenck

The merit of supporting Torah is very great.

This book has been made possible in part

by the generosity of

Sylvia and William Poe.

Thank you.

The merit of supporting Torah is very great.

This book has been made possible in part

by the generosity of

Jack and Lisa Fishman.

Thank you.

The merit of supporting Torah is very great.

This book has been made possible in part

by the generosity of

Charles Deutsch.

Thank you.

The merit of supporting Torah is very great.

This book has been made possible in part

by the generosity of

James Pollock

*

Emily Grafman

*

Don Singer

*

And

Sonia Gilbert

The merit of supporting Torah is very great.

Special thanks also to the generosity of

Lon Bliss

Lisa Fulsom

Kirk Gaton

Robert Kestelik

Anna Lanis

Candace Lowenstein

Ellen Paster

David Schwartz

Joan Silber

Nancy Stein

Ray Rosenthal

And

Chanoch and Yocheved Turner

Printed in the United States
24887LVS00001B/269